The iPhone
PocketGuide
Sixth Edition

Christopher**Breen**

Ginormous knowledge, pocket-sized.

**Peachpit
Press**

The iPhone Pocket Guide, Sixth Edition

Christopher Breen

Peachpit Press
1249 Eighth Street
Berkeley, CA 94710
510/524-2178
510/524-2221 (fax)

Find us on the Web at: www.peachpit.com
To report errors, please send a note to errata@peachpit.com.

Peachpit Press is a division of Pearson Education.

Executive editor: Clifford Colby
Editor: Kathy Simpson
Production editor: David Van Ness
Compositor: WolfsonDesign
Indexer: Valerie Haynes Perry
Cover Design: RHDG / Riezebos Holzbaur Design Group, Peachpit Press
Interior Design: Peachpit Press
Logo Design: MINE™ (www.minesf.com)

Notice of Rights

Notice of Liability

Trademarks

ISBN-13 978-0-321-81411-1
ISBN-10   0-321-81411-8

9 8 7 6 5 4 3 2 1

Printed and bound in the United States of America

To Steve Jobs, without whom I'd likely still be working in a darkened piano lounge.

About the Author

Christopher Breen has been writing about Apple technology since the latter days of the Reagan administration for such publications as *MacUser*, *MacWEEK*, and *Macworld*. Currently a senior editor with *Macworld*, he pens the popular *Mac 911* blog and column, and hosts the *Macworld Podcast*. A popular speaker, he also has many training titles available from Lynda.com, including *Mac OS X Lion Essential Training*, *iPad Tips and Tricks*, and *Screencasting for the Mac*. When not engaged in writing, Mr. Breen is a professional musician in Northern California.

Acknowledgments

This book would not be in your hands (or, if you're that sort of person, on your e-book reader) if not for the dedication of the following people.

At Peachpit Press: Publisher Nancy Ruenzel, who continues to support these efforts; Cliff Colby, who started the ball rolling with the offer to write this series of guides; Kathy Simpson, who, as usual, did everything that needed doing after the manuscript left my computer and took up residence on hers; production pro David Van Ness, who, with barely an anxious ripple, turned our work into the lovely book you hold now; WolfsonDesign, which made words and pictures fit so attractively within the confines of these pages; and Valerie Haynes Perry, who performed a book's most thankless yet necessary job: indexing.

At home: My wife, Claire, and daughter, Addie, who gave me supportive hugs at the end of each working day (and the occasional free day too).

Abroad: *Macworld* Editorial Director Jason Snell, who never said, "I'd like exclusive rights to that brain full of iPhone goodness" and the boys from System 9 for their continued cool-cattedness.

And, of course, the sleep-deprived designers, engineers, and other Apple folk who gave birth to the iPhone and iPod touch and the software that runs them, and the countless developers who make these devices more wonderful hunks of technology with each passing day.

Contents

1

Meet the iPhone and iPod touch

Allow me to lead off this pocketable guide with this crucial advice regarding the iPhone and iPod touch: *Don't be fooled by the names.* By that, I mean that although the names indicate that the iPhone is little more than a mobile phone and the iPod touch must be primarily a media player, the truth is that each device is a small but very powerful, very flexible mobile computer.

The iPhone additionally happens to make and receive phone calls, but that's just one of its many talents. In fact, both devices offer all these features:

Email client	Calendar
Web browser	Address book
Camera	Text editor
Music and video player	Book and magazine reader
Text messaging	Weather
Maps and GPS	Stock ticker
Photo viewer	To-do reminders
Clock (alarm clock, stopwatch, timer, world clock)	Game player

And, as they say in the cartoons, that ain't all. Thanks to the more than half-*million* apps available through Apple's App Store, your iPhone or iPod touch can be just about anything you want it to be. Best of all, it works with both Windows PCs and Macs, and the software necessary to sync it with your computer and the world at large is a program that you likely already have on your computer: Apple's iTunes.

The iPhone and iPod touch have far more commonalities than differences. Because they're so similar, I've chosen to discuss both in a book that could just have easily been titled *The iPhone **and iPod touch** Pocket Guide*. So, lucky you, you get two books for the price of one.

In this inaugural chapter, I look at the items that come in the iPhone and iPod touch boxes, as well as the physical features and controls that make up these marvelous devices.

Boxed In

The box holds more than just the iPhone or iPod touch. Within, you'll find these goodies.

iPhone or iPod touch

Well, of course. You didn't lay out your hard-earned cash for a box stuffed with gravel. Open the box, and there's your iPhone or iPod touch.

Stereo headset

Each of these devices includes a stereo headset, but the headsets aren't identical, though they look quite similar. The difference is that the iPhone's headset includes a small microphone and switch that's attached to the cable dangling from the right earbud. This stereo headset, with its onboard microphone, not only frees your hands for playing with the iPhone's other features, but also lets you listen to your favorite tunes; serves as an audio aid when you're watching a video; and (if you have an iPhone 3GS or iPhone 4) allows you, through Voice Control, to demand that your phone dial a friend or play the catalog of a favorite artist. (If you have an iPhone 4S and Siri—the iPhone's voice-controlled intelligent assistant—you can demand a whole lot more.)

Here's how you use the headset on both devices:

- To adjust the volume, press the top of the switch to increase volume or the bottom of the switch to turn things down. These volume buttons aren't of the press-and-hold variety. Volume goes up or down only when you press and release the button. To increase volume by two increments, press the top button twice in succession.

- While listening to music or watching a video, press the switch once in the middle to pause playback.

- Press it twice to move to the next track when listening to music. To fast-forward, press twice and hold.

- Press it three times in succession to move to the previous track when listening to music. To rewind, press three times and hold.

- Press the switch twice in rapid succession while you're watching a video, and if the video has chapter markers, you skip to the next chapter. (If the video has no chapters, nothing happens.) If you press three times in rapid succession while watching a video with chapters, you move back to the beginning of the currently playing chapter. Stop playback with a single click and press the switch three times quickly, and you go back to the previous chapter.

And here's how you use the headset on an iPhone:

- When the phone rings, press it once to answer the call and again to end the call.

- To decline a call, press and hold for a couple of seconds; then let go. The iPhone beeps twice to acknowledge your action.

- While you're in the middle of a call, press once to answer an incoming call and put the first call on hold.

- To end the current call and answer an incoming call or switch to a call on hold, press and hold for 2 seconds; then let go.

- If you have an iPhone 3GS or iPhone 4, and you're not in the middle of a call, press and hold the center of the switch for a couple of seconds to call up the Voice Control screen. If you have an iPhone 4S, this same action calls up Siri.

tip You can also use the iPhone's headset to control many of these same functions on an iPod touch. You can't make traditional phone calls on the touch, of course, but you can use the microphone with VoIP applications such as Skype, as well as use the volume buttons and switch to control media playback and Voice Control.

Documentation

Inside the paper envelope beneath the plastic tray are three hunks of paper: Finger Tips, a short guide to using your iPhone or iPod touch (unnecessary, as you're holding this much larger guide); a safety information guide, which you may be able to read if you wear 6x reading glasses; and a sheet that bears two white Apple stickers, appropriate for placing anywhere you want to let your Apple flag fly.

USB power adapter (iPhone only)

Apple bundles in a power adapter that looks very much like those three-prong-to-two-prong plug adapters that you find at the local hardware store. On one side are the two blades you plug into a power outlet; on the other is a USB port into which you plug the device's dock connector-to-USB cable.

Dock connector-to-USB cable

Speaking of that cable, this is the one you string between the dock-connector port on the bottom of the iPhone or iPod touch and either the USB power adapter or a USB port on your computer. When it's connected to a computer, this cable acts as both data and power link between the device and computer. Even if you choose to sync your device over Wi-Fi, you'll need this cable the first time you set up syncing, as well as whenever you want to charge the device.

On the Face of It

Thanks to its touchscreen display, the iPhone and iPod touch sport very few buttons and switches. Those that they do possess, however, are important, as you see in **Figure 1.1** and **Figure 1.2**.

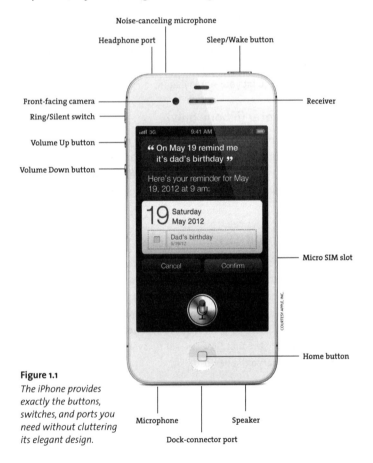

Figure 1.1

The iPhone provides exactly the buttons, switches, and ports you need without cluttering its elegant design.

Front-facing camera   Sleep/Wake switch

Volume Up button

Volume Down button

Home button

Figure 1.2
*The 4G iPod touch
features fewer controls.*

Dock-connector port   Headphone port

COURTESY APPLE, INC.

Up front

After peeling the plastic off your iPhone or iPod touch and flipping it in your hand a time or two, you'll come to a remarkable realization: The thing apparently has but one button on the front! No number keys, no tiny joystick, no Answer and Hang Up buttons—just an indented round button at the bottom of the display. This button is the Home button, and as its name implies, it takes you to the device's Home screen nearly every time you click it once.

(OK, I'll end the suspense: You also use the Home button to wake up your sleeping iPhone or iPod touch. When you do, you don't go Home; rather, after unlocking the thing, you see the last screen that was visible when the phone dozed off. Also, when you click this button while you're already looking at the first page of the Home screen, you're taken to the Spotlight screen, where you can search for items on your iPhone or iPod touch.)

Clicking twice in rapid succession does one of two things:

- If the iPhone or iPod touch is asleep, doing this takes you to a lock screen that shows both controls for playing music and a Camera button that you can use to take a picture quickly with the device.

- If the iPhone or iPod touch is awake, double-click this button, and the Home screen slides up to reveal a palette of recently used apps.

Unlike iPod touches, all iPhones bear a small slit near the top. This slit is the *receiver*—the hole through which you listen to the person you're speaking with when you operate the phone in traditional phone-to-face mode. Both the iPhone and iPod touch offer a front-facing camera next to the receiver. I discuss the cameras at length in Chapter 8.

On top

Look a little more carefully, and you discover a few more mechanical controls and ports. On the top edge of the iPhone and iPod touch is a tiny switch. Apple describes this switch as the Sleep/Wake button, which you also use to turn the device on and off.

To lock the phone or iPod, press this button. (To unlock it, click the Home button and slide your finger where you see the words *Slide to Unlock*.) To switch the device off, press and hold the Sleep/Wake button for a few seconds until a red slider, labeled Slide to Power Off, appears onscreen. Drag the slider to the right to switch off the device (or tap Cancel to belay that order). "Drag?" you ask. Yes, the gesture is exactly what it sounds like. Place your finger on the arrow button and slide it to the right. (I describe all these maneuvers in the "Full Gestures" section later in this chapter.)

To turn the iPhone or iPod touch on after shutting it off, press and hold the Sleep/Wake button until you see the Apple logo on the display.

Hunkered down in the top-left corner of all of today's iPhones is the Headphone port, which accommodates the iPhone's white headset plug. The iPod touch's headphone port is located on the bottom of the device.

Next to the Headphone port on the iPhone 4 and iPhone 4S is a small hole, which is the iPhone's noise-canceling microphone. The idea is that if you're on a call in a noisy environment, this microphone will pick up the ambient noise around you and—using sophisticated circuitry inside the device—filter out that noise.

Down below

Smack-dab in the middle of the iPhone's and iPod touch's bottom edge is the familiar-to-iPod-owners dock-connector port. This port is a proprietary 30-pin connector used for initially syncing and always powering the iPhone and iPod touch, as well as attaching such accessories as power adapters and speaker systems.

The opening in the bottom-left corner of the iPhone 4 and iPhone 4S is for the device's built-in microphone. The hole in the bottom-right corner is for the phone's speaker.

The microphone and speaker ports are reversed on the iPhone 3G and 3GS.

On the side

The left sides of the iPhone and iPod touch differ in that though each device has Volume Up and Volume Down buttons, the iPhone additionally has a switch that you use to silence the phone. When the switch is toggled toward the face of the phone, the iPhone is in the Ring position. Push the switch toward the back of the phone to silence the ringer. That orange bar you see when the switch is pushed toward the back of the phone tells you that it's in the Silent position. To mute the iPod touch, push and hold its Volume Down button.

You'll find the volume control(s) below the Ring/Silent switch. On iPhones before the iPhone 4, volume is controlled by a single toggle switch. Press that switch up to increase the volume of a call, song, or video; press it down to decrease the volume. On the iPhone 4 and iPhone 4S, Apple provides separate round volume buttons: the top Volume Up (+) button to increase volume and the bottom Volume Down (–) button to decrease volume.

On the right side of the iPhone 4 and iPhone 4S is the micro SIM (Subscriber Information Module) slot. Within this slot is a card holding a programmable circuit board that stores your personal subscriber information. This card allows the iPhone to work. Without it, you've got a phone that can't make or receive calls, or send or receive SMS messages. Unlike some other mobile phones, the iPhone comes with this removable card preinstalled. The iPod touch doesn't have a SIM card of any variety.

The back

On the back of the iPhone 4 and iPhone 4S, you'll find both the rear-facing camera lens and the LED flash. The iPod touch also has a camera on the back. It doesn't bear a flash, but does have a tiny microphone port just to the right of the camera lens.

Apps

The iPhone and iPod touch are remarkably capable devices right out of the box because of the apps bundled with them. I take a look at them all in this section.

The Big Four

Apple configures these devices so that the most important apps—in Apple's estimation—appear in the Dock. The Big Four differ on the iPhone and iPod touch because the iPod isn't a phone. Here's how they shake out on each device.

Phone (iPhone only)

Tap the Phone icon on the Home screen, and you're taken to the main Phone screen, where you can make calls, pull up a list of your contacts, view recent calls, and listen to your voice mail. I describe this area in rich detail in Chapter 3.

Mail

This application is the iPhone's and iPod touch's email client. As with the email client on your computer, you use the Mail app to compose and send messages, as well as to read and manage received email. I look at Mail in Chapter 4.

Safari

Safari is Apple's Web browser. Unlike many other mobile devices, the iPhone and iPod touch carry a real-live Web browser rather than a "baby browser" that grudgingly allows you to view only a small portion of the material that a Web page offers. When you pull up a Web page in the Safari app, it looks and behaves like a real Web page. Chapter 5 is devoted to Safari.

Music

Perhaps the coolest music player ever made is incorporated into your iPhone and iPod touch. Capable of playing both audio and video, the iPhone and iPod touch are wonderful on-the-go media players. Look to Chapter 6 for the ins and outs of the music and video functions.

Messages

As I said, the Big Four differs on the two devices. Although both the iPhone and iPod touch have the Messages app, only the iPod touch has it installed in the Dock by default. Messages is Apple's text-messaging application, which I discuss in Chapter 3.

note As I write this chapter, the iBooks app isn't bundled with the iPhone or iPod touch but is available as a free download from the App Store. Still, it's important enough to mention here.

The others

The built-in applications don't stop with the Big Four and the store apps. The iPhone and iPod touch also include other applications that handle things like reminders, calendars, contacts, stocks, and weather.

FaceTime (iPod touch only)

The iPhone 4S, iPhone 4, and 4G iPod touch are capable of making video calls using Apple's FaceTime technology. Only the iPod touch has a separate FaceTime app, as the iPhone has FaceTime built into the Phone app. Find out all about FaceTime in Chapter 3.

Calendar

When you sync your iPhone or iPod touch to either your computer or to iCloud (Apple's online syncing service), you can transfer calendar events and alarms from Apple's iCal and from Microsoft's Outlook. If you have an iCloud, Yahoo, Gmail, AOL, Hotmail, or Microsoft Exchange account, you can sync the calendar information from these services automatically over the air. These transferred and synced items appear in the Calendar app. You can also add events directly to the iPhone or iPod touch by using the keyboard and then sync those events with your computer or one of the services I just mentioned.

Additionally, if you have an iPhone 4S, you can create calendar events with Siri (which I talk about later in this chapter). I discuss Calendar in more detail in Chapter 4.

Photos

Tap the Photos icon, and you see a list of photo albums—the first holding the pictures you've taken with the device's camera, the next containing those imported via Photo Stream (an iCloud feature), and another that contains all the images on the device, followed by any albums or folders you've synced with the iPhone or iPod touch. Chapter 8 offers more details on both devices' photo capabilities.

Camera

Use this application to snap a picture with the built-in camera. On the iPhone and iPod touch, you can also shoot and edit videos with the Camera app. The camera, photos, and movies shot with the iPhone and iPod touch are the subjects of Chapter 8.

Videos

As its name implies, the Videos app is where you watch videos that you've synced to your iPhone or iPod touch, or that are available to it through iTunes Home Sharing, which I discuss in Chapter 6.

YouTube

With this application, you can view streamed YouTube videos on your iPhone or iPod touch or are available through iTunes Home Sharing, which I discuss in Chapter 6.

Maps

Lost? A street map is just a tap away. Based on Google Maps, this application quickly provides not only maps, but also current driving conditions, satellite views, the locations of businesses within each map, and GPS and directional information. Chapter 9 covers the Maps app.

Weather

Much like a Mac OS X widget, the Weather application displays current conditions, as well as the six-day and hourly forecasts for locations of your choosing. Like I said, Chapter 9 is great.

Notes

Notes is the iPhone's and iPod touch's tiny text editor. Use the virtual keyboard (or use the iPhone 4S's dictation capabilities) to create lists, jot down reminders, compose haiku, or remind yourself to look in Chapter 9 for more details.

Reminders

With iOS 5, to-do notes—which Apple calls *reminders*—finally come to the iPhone and iPod touch. Reminders are more than simple checklists; they're to-do lists that can pop to the fore based on your location. Find out more about reminders in Chapter 4.

Clock

The Clock app lets you find the time anywhere in the world, as well as create clocks for favorite locations. You also use the Clock application to create alarms and to invoke the stopwatch and countdown timer. I talk Clock in Chapter 9.

Game Center

Gamers like to get together not only to play against or with each other, but also to brag about their achievements. Game Center is the social service provided by Apple that lets them do these things. This topic is another one for Chapter 9.

Newsstand

Newsstand is a gathering place for any periodicals—newspapers and magazines—that you subscribe to via apps available from the App Store. I give Newsstand its due in Chapter 9.

Stocks

Similar to the Stocks widget in Apple's Mac OS X, the Stocks app lets you track your favorite stocks in near real time. All widgety things are detailed in Chapter 9.

Utilities

Since iOS 4, Apple has ganged together a few apps in a Utilities folder. In iOS 5, this folder contains three or four apps, depending on whether you have an iPhone or iPod touch: Contacts, Calculator, Compass (iPhone only), and Voice Memos.

Contacts is the iPhone's and iPod touch's address book. This app is where you create and manage your contacts, which other apps (such as Mail) draw on. I talk about contacts in Chapter 3.

Calculator is for performing common math operations—and, with the Scientific Calculator view that appears when you turn the device to a horizontal position, not-so-common math operations too. See Chapter 9.

Compass (iPhone only) is the most visible example of the iPhone's magnetometer, which tells the iPhone the direction in which it's pointing—northeast or southwest, for example. To glean this kind of information, tap the Compass app to view...well, a compass. Set it for Chapter 9.

Voice Memos lets you record audio through the iPhone's or iPod touch's microphone and play it back through the speaker or the Headphone port. Again, see Chapter 9.

Settings

A tap of the Settings icon produces a preferences window for configuring many of the iPhone's and iPod touch's functions. Some third-party applications plant their settings in this screen as well. Though I discuss Settings in regard to specific applications throughout this little tome, I provide the big picture in Chapter 2.

Housekeeping

Far too many people purchase an iPhone or iPod touch, download an app or two, then a few more, and then lots more, and before they know it, they're flicking from page to page trying to find that elusive Classic Cooking for Zombies app. They do this because they're unaware of their device's organizational talents. Apple provides two good ways to keep your iPhone and iPod touch organized: the customized Home screen and folders.

Customizing the Home screen

The positions of icons on the Home screen aren't ordained by the heavens. You're welcome to move icons where you like. On the iPhone and iPod touch, this is easy to do. Follow these steps:

1. Tap and hold any icon.

All the icons on the Home screen start to wiggle.

2. Drag the icon to a new position.

When you drag an icon, other icons get out of its way to make room for it. You can move an icon to another screen simply by dragging it to the edge of the screen. If you drag an icon to the right side, it moves to the next screen; if you drag an icon to the left, it moves to the preceding screen.

You can also drag apps out of the Dock. If you rarely surf the Web with Safari, for example, drag its icon out, and replace it with a different app.

3. Let go.

Take your finger off the icon, and the app takes up residence where you dropped it. To stop all the wiggling, just click the Home button.

tip You can also delete third-party apps from your device while they're wiggling. (You can't delete Apple's bundled apps.) Just tap the X that appears in the top-left corner of an app's icon to delete it.

Alternatively, you can sync your device with your computer, launch iTunes (if it doesn't launch automatically), select the iPhone or iPod touch in iTunes' Source list, click the Apps tab, and use the onscreen representation of the Home screen to rearrange icons. I discuss this feature in detail in Chapter 2.

Organizing with folders

Rearranging icons is all well and good, but if you have a couple hundred apps on your iPhone or iPod touch, you're still going to flail a bit, regardless of how organized the icons are. Fortunately, Apple offers a second way to tidy your device's Home screen: folders. Just as you can drop items into folders on your computer, you can place items in folders on your iPhone running iOS 4 or later. Again, this is easy to do, like so:

1. Tap and hold an app icon that you want to add to a folder.

Once again, all the icons on the Home screen jitter.

2. Drag the app icon on top of another app icon of the same type to create a folder.

Suppose that you want to organize your games in a folder. To do so, tap and hold, say, Super Bouncy Pudding Time, and drag it on top of Marsupial Madness. The Home screen fades, and a bar appears that contains the two app icons.

3. Name your folder.

The device identifies the first app by its type—a game, in this example—and automatically names the folder Games. You can keep the name or tap the small X in the Name field and type a name you like.

4. Tap the Home screen to create the folder.

The new folder and other icons on the Home screen continue to wiggle, which indicates that you can reposition the folder by dragging it to a new location.

5. Add more items.

Before you stop all the shaking, drag other likely icons on top of your folder. Each folder can hold up to 12 apps.

6. Click the Home button to stop the motion.

7. Admire your work.

Tap your new folder to reveal its contents (**Figure 1.3**).

Figure 1.3
The contents of a folder.

Notification Center

Another feature introduced with iOS 5 is Notification Center, a handy place to view tidbits of information such as the local weather, stock prices, email subject headings, Twitter messages addressed to you, text messages, reminders, and calendar events.

Notification Center makes its presence known in a couple of ways. The first is on the lock screen. If you've configured notifications to appear here (I discuss how to do this in Chapter 2), when you unlock your iPhone or iPod touch by clicking the Home button when the device is asleep, you'll see short notifications: calendar events scheduled for that day, for example, or the first bit of an email message you've received.

To see a more complete list of notifications, unlock your device, tap the time at the very top of the screen, and swipe down. When you do, your notifications appear (**Figure 1.4**).

Figure 1.4
*Weather,
Reminders,
Calendar,
and Stocks
notifications
in Notification
Center.*

By default, you see local weather information and a stock ticker that displays common indexes such as the Dow Jones Industrial Average and NASDAQ. If you've chosen to display other notifications (again, Chapter 2 tells you how), they appear on this screen as well. In many cases, you can act on a notification by tapping it. Tap a calendar event to view the event in the Calendars app; tap an email message, and the device's Mail app opens, displaying the entire message.

Some notifications, such as reminders and email messages, disappear from Notification Center when you tap them. Others, such as calendar events, remain. If you want to clear an individual notification or any of the same variety, just tap the X that appears next to a notification heading—Mail, for example. A Clear button appears. Tap it, and all the notification of that particular kind disappear from Notification Center. The original items (in this case, email messages) aren't erased from the device—just their notifications.

Full Gestures

The iPhone's and iPod touch's screen is deliberately touchy: Touching it is how you control the device. This section covers the gestures you use to navigate and control your device.

Tap

You're going to see the word *tap* a lot in this book. When you want to initiate an action—launch an app, control the music playback features, flip an object around, or move to the next screen—this gesture is the one you'll likely use. If you've turned on the iPhone's or iPod touch's VoiceOver accessibility feature, which helps the visually and aurally impaired use the device, a single tap selects an item. I cover accessibility in Chapter 2.

Tap and hold

You use the tap-and-hold gesture when editing text—either to bring up the magnifying-glass icon to help insert a cursor or to initiate the process of cutting, copying, and pasting text. See "Text Entry and Editing" later in this chapter for more on cutting, copying, and pasting.

Double tap

Sometimes, just one tap won't do. Double-tapping often enlarges or contracts an image—zooms in on a photo or Web-page column, for example, or returns it to its normal size after you've enlarged it. At other times, it can make items return to the previous view.

When the VoiceOver feature is on, a double tap acts like a single tap ordinarily does. With VoiceOver engaged, one tap tells you what you're touching, and a double tap launches the application or item you want to use.

If you engage the Zoom feature—another accessibility option—a double tap with three fingers zooms the display.

Flick

If you want to scroll up or down a long list rapidly on your device, zip through a selection of album covers in Cover Flow view (a view that allows you to browse your music and podcast collection by album cover/artwork), or flip from one photo to another, you use the flick gesture. As you flick faster, the iPhone or iPod touch attempts to match your action by scrolling or zipping more rapidly. Slower flicks produce less motion on the display.

To stop the motion initiated by a flick, just place your finger on the display. Motion stops instantly.

Two-finger flick

If you've downloaded Apple's Remote app from the App Store (a wonderful application for controlling iTunes remotely on your computer or on Apple TV), you'll find that when you're controlling an Apple TV device, a two-finger flick to the left causes a video playing on Apple TV to back up 10 seconds.

Drag

For finer control, drag your finger across the display. Use this motion to scroll in a controlled way down a list or email message, or to reposition an enlarged image or Web page. You also drag the volume slider and playhead when you're in the Music and Videos apps.

Three-finger flick

By default, the three-finger flick is used only when VoiceOver is on. In that situation, this gesture is used for scrolling.

Three-finger drag

By default, this multifinger gesture works only with the Zoom accessibility feature. When Zoom is on, a three-finger drag moves the screen so that you can see the parts hidden by the zoom.

Rotor

Rotor is another special gesture reserved for use when VoiceOver is turned on. You place two fingers on the iPhone's or iPod touch's screen and then turn them as though you're turning a dial. I talk more about this gesture when I discuss accessibility in Chapter 2.

Stretch/pinch

To expand an image, such as a photo or Web page, place your thumb and index finger together on the display and then stretch them apart. To make an image smaller, start with your thumb and finger apart and then pinch them together.

Touch and drag

You use this gesture when you want to change the positions of icons or put items in a folder. Tap and hold icons on the Home screen, for example, and they start wiggling, indicating that they can be moved. Touch and drag an icon to move it to a different place, or touch and drag it to the edge of the screen to move it to another Home-screen page. To create a folder, tap and drag an icon atop another icon. In the Music app's More section, for example, you'll find the option to swap out icons along the bottom of the display by tapping the Edit button and then touching and dragging new icons into place.

Multitasking

Multitasking lets your iPhone or iPod touch perform chores like play music in the background as you work in another app. It also lets you switch away from one app, move to another, and switch back to that first app without losing your work in either app.

Multitasking works this way:

1. Double-click the Home button.

The Home screen scoots up, the icons fade, and a new Dock appears at the bottom of the display. In this Dock are the apps that you've used most recently (**Figure 1.5**).

Figure 1.5
The multitasking Dock.

2. Tap an app to switch to it.

The device uses a revolving-door effect to rotate from the currently open application to the new application you've chosen.

3. Double-click the Home button again.

To return to the preceding app or choose a different app, just double-click the Home button again and then tap the app. The last app you used appears in the first position. If you don't see the app you want, flick the Dock to the left or right. Additional apps appear.

More on the Multitasking Dock

The multitasking Dock has some hidden powers. Flick it to the right, and you'll see controls for playing music in the Music app as well as the Rotation Lock icon (**Figure 1.6**). Tap the Music icon, and that app launches. Choose the music you like, and it plays. (See Chapter 6 for more on playing media with your iPhone or iPod touch.) From the multitasking Dock, you can pause playback as well as use the Back/ Rewind and Next/ Fast-Forward buttons to do their respective jobs.

Figure 1.6
The Music controls and Rotation Lock icon in the multitasking Dock.

Tap the Rotation Lock icon, and the device's display remains in portrait orientation regardless of how you hold it.

tip To force-quit an app and remove it from the multitasking Dock—something you may want to do if an app has locked up—just tap and hold it until it starts to wiggle. Tap the red Delete button, and the app disappears from the Dock (but not from the Home screen).

Text Entry and Editing

Taps, pinches, and drags help you navigate the iPhone and iPod touch, but they won't compose email messages for you, correct spelling mistakes, or delete ill-considered complaints. The keyboard and a well-placed finger will do these jobs. If you have an iPhone 4S, however, you may be able to dispense with the keyboard and simply dictate the words you want the device to write. In this section, I start with the keyboard.

Touch typing

The iPhone's and iPod touch's virtual keyboard largely matches the configuration of your computer's keyboard. You'll find an alphabetic layout when you open most applications (**Figure 1.7**).

Figure 1.7
An iPhone's keyboard.

To capitalize characters, tap the up-arrow key (the device's Shift key). To view numbers and most punctuation characters, tap the 123 key (iPhone 4S) or .?123 key (iPhone 4 and iPod touch). To see less-used characters (including £, ¥, and €), choose the number layout by tapping the numbers key and then tapping the #+= key. The Space, Return, and Delete keys do exactly what you'd expect. You can produce alternative characters, such as those with accents or umlauts, by tapping and holding the most appropriate character and then waiting for a pop-up menu of characters to appear. Tap and hold the letter *E*, for example, and you get a menu that includes such characters as *è, é, ê,* and *ë.*

To make typing easier, the keyboard's layout changes depending on the application you're using. In Mail, for example, the bottom row holds the at symbol (@), along with a period (.). Tap and hold that period key, and a pop-up menu displays .net, .edu, .org, .us, and .com; append these extensions simply by sliding your finger over the one you want and then pulling your finger away. While you're working in Safari, the default layout shows period (.), slash (/), and .com keys along the bottom. Tap and hold the .com key to see a pop-up menu that also includes .net, .edu, .us, .org, and .us.

tip When you type a character, its magnified image appears as you touch it. If you tap the wrong character, leave your finger where it is and slide it to the character you want; the character won't be "typed" until you let go of it.

Speaking the speech

If you have an iPhone 4S, you're excused from a fair bit of touch typing. With supported apps such as Notes, Messages, and Mail, your phone can transcribe your speech. For transcription to work, you must switch Siri on, which you do from the Home screen by tapping General > Siri.

Give Siri a try now, using Notes as an example:

1. Launch the Notes app.

2. Tap the plus (+) button to create a new note.

Notice the small microphone button to the left of the spacebar.

3. Tap the microphone button.

A gray bar bearing the image of a microphone appears at the bottom of the screen.

4. Say "The quick brown dog comma who belongs to Farmer Brown comma jumped over the lazy dog period."

5. Tap Done.

6. Gawk as your words—complete with punctuation—appear in your note.

> **note** You'll notice that your words *comma* and *period* weren't spelled out, but used as punctuation. That's how speech technology like Siri works. You have to specifically define the punctuation and formatting you want to use. If you want to place a line break between sentences, for example, say "New paragraph."

Examining text

The iPhone and iPod touch offer a unique way to edit text. You needn't tap the Delete key time and again to work your way back to your mistake. Instead, tap and hold the line of text you want to edit. When you do, a magnifying glass appears (**Figure 1.8**), showing a close-up view of the area under your finger. Inside this magnified view is a blinking cursor. Drag the cursor to where you want to make your correction—after the word or letter you want to correct—and then tap the Delete key to remove the text. In most cases, you can also tap between words to insert the cursor there.

Figure 1.8
Tap and hold to magnify text and insert the cursor.

Cutting, copying, and pasting

Just as you can on your computer, you can select, cut, copy, and paste text (and copy and paste graphics) on your iPhone or iPod touch.

Editing text

To select text for later cutting, copying, or replacing, tap and hold near the text you want to select. A balloon appears that includes the words *Select* and *Select All*. To select the word closest to the cursor, tap Select. To select everything on the page, tap Select All.

When you do either of these things, the balloon changes to display the words *Cut* and *Copy* (and possibly *Paste* if something's in the device's clipboard). If you've selected a single word, you may also see *Suggest* and (when you tap the right-pointing arrow) *Define*. In either case, the text is highlighted in blue, and blue handles appear at the beginning and end of the text (**Figure 1.9**).

Figure 1.9
*With a couple
of taps, you can
cut, copy, paste,
or replace words
on your iPhone or
iPod touch.*

To alter the size of the selection, just drag the handles. When you've
selected what you want, tap Cut to make the selected text disappear and
add it to the device's clipboard (a virtual holding area for storing cut and
copied items). Tap Copy to leave the text where it is but also place a copy
of it on the clipboard. You tap Suggest when a word is misspelled and
you're looking for three spelling alternatives. Tapping Define causes the
device's dictionary to appear, providing the selected word's definition.

To paste material on the clipboard, just tap somewhere to place the
insertion cursor; tap that cursor; and then select Paste, which now
appears in the balloon along with Select and Select All.

Siri (iPhone 4S Only)

Siri—the voice-controlled intelligent assistant—is the marquee feature
of the iPhone 4S. "Exactly what is a voice-controlled intelligent assistant?", you may ask. Essentially, it lets you ask your iPhone for information or instruct it to perform a particular task, and then it complies in a
helpful way.

To use Siri, simply click and hold the Home button until you hear a double
"boink" sound. The screen fades to gray, a microphone icon appears at the

bottom of the screen, and the words *What can I help you with?* appear above this icon. Tap the icon, and start talking. Here are a few examples:

Me: *What time is it?*

Siri: *At the tone, the time will be 8:39 a.m.* (Siri shows a clock with the local time.)

Me: *Remind me to call my wife at 4 p.m.* (**Figure 1.10**).

Figure 1.10
I've told Siri who my wife is so it can create a reminder with her name.

Siri: *OK, I'll remind you.* (Siri creates a reminder item.)

Me: *Schedule lunch with Ben Long tomorrow at Taco Gordo.*

Siri: *OK, here's your meeting. Note that you already have 2 meetings that overlap with this. Shall I schedule this anyway?*

Me: *No, move my lunch date with Ben to Friday.*

Siri: *All right, the meeting with Ben Long is on your calendar for this Friday.*

Me: *Who is my uncle?*

Siri: *What is your uncle's name?*

Me: *Fred Breen.*

Siri: *OK, do you want me to remember that Fred Breen is your uncle?*

Me: *Yes.*

Siri: *OK, Christopher, I've added this relationship. Here's the contact information.* (Siri tags Fred Breen as my uncle so that I can later command "Call my uncle" or "Email my uncle," and Siri will know who I'm talking about.)

Me: *What's $100 in Australian dollars?*

Siri: *OK, here you go.* (A graph appears with the result $97.70, which was the correct answer for that particular day.)

Me: *Who's the president of Slovenia?*

Siri: *Danilo Türk.*

I could go on and on, but you get the idea. Siri can not only perform tasks on the iPhone (such as creating reminders, calendar events, email messages, and contacts), but also search the Internet for information. Also, as with the far-less-capable Voice Control feature on the iPhone 4 and iPod touch, it can dial phone numbers and play music at your command.

An exhaustive list of what Siri can do would be...well, exhausting, and this feature is only going to get more powerful over time. My best advice is to play with Siri and see what it responds to. As you explore, you'll discover that Siri has an attitude. Swear at it, for example, and it snarks right back at you.

note Siri can be operated from the iPhone's lock screen—which, while convenient, means that anyone who picks up your phone can manipulate it, which isn't good. To prevent this possibility, tap Settings >

General > Passcode Lock. Tap Turn Passcode On; enter and confirm a passcode; and then, in the Passcode Lock screen, turn Siri off.

Icon See That

When you're operating your iPhone or iPod touch, you'll see a variety of small icons in its status bar. Here's what they mean:

⚊ıll   **Cell signal (iPhone only).** This icon indicates how strong a signal your phone is receiving. The more bars you see, the better the signal. If you're out of range of your carrier's network, you'll see *No Service.*

✈   **Airplane mode.** All functions that broadcast a signal—making a call, using Wi-Fi or EDGE networks, connecting to Bluetooth devices, and so on—are shut off when you switch the phone to airplane mode.

📶   **Wi-Fi.** This icon indicates that you're connected to a Wi-Fi network. The stronger the signal, the more bars you see.

3G   **3G (iPhone only).** If 3G is available to your phone, this icon appears.

E   **EDGE (iPhone only).** This icon indicates that you're within range of your carrier's EDGE network.

O   **GPRS (iPhone only).** The iPhone supports General Packet Radio Service, a data-moving technology on GSM (for Global System for Mobile communication) networks that's more common outside the United States. If your carrier offers GPRS (as AT&T does), and its GPRS network is available, you see this symbol.

(Continues on next page)

Icon See That (continued)

Personal Hotspot (iPhone only). By paying your phone carrier something extra each month ($20 for AT&T), you can use your iPhone as a wireless hotspot, to which you can connect other devices for accessing the Internet. This symbol indicates that you've enabled the hotspot.

Syncing. This symbol appears when your iPhone or iPod touch is syncing with your computer.

VPN. The iPhone and iPod touch display this symbol if you're connected to a virtual private network.

Network activity. If your device is busy talking to a network, you see the Mac OS X–like "I'm doing something" symbol.

Call forwarding (iPhone only). If you've turned on call forwarding for your phone (a feature that I discuss in Chapter 3), this symbol appears.

Lock. Your device is locked.

Play. Your device is playing music.

Portrait orientation lock. You can lock the iPhone and iPod touch so that when they're rotated, the screen doesn't rotate from portrait to landscape orientation. When the lock is engaged, this symbol appears.

Alarm. You've set an alarm.

Location Services. When an app is using Location Services to pinpoint your position—as Maps does—you see this symbol.

(Continues on next page)

Icon See That (continued)

Bluetooth. If you see a blue or white Bluetooth icon, the device is linked to a Bluetooth device. If you see a gray Bluetooth icon, Bluetooth is on, but the iPhone or iPod touch isn't linked to a Bluetooth device.

Battery. This icon indicates the battery level and charging status. A battery icon with a lightning bolt tells you that the device is charging. When you see a battery icon with a plug icon, the battery is connected to a power supply and fully charged. A battery icon without a lightning-bolt or plug icon tells you that the iPhone or iPod touch isn't plugged into power. The solid portion of the battery icon tells you approximately how much power is left in the battery. If, on an iPhone 3GS, iPhone 4, or iPhone 4S, you've switched on the Battery Percentage feature (tap Settings > General > Usage), you'll see the percentage of remaining battery charge—94%, for example—listed to the left of the battery icon.

Bluetooth battery. If you've paired a supported Bluetooth device (such as a keyboard) with your iPhone or iPod touch, this symbol indicates its remaining charge.

TTY (iPhone only). If the iPhone is configured to work with a TTY device, this symbol appears. (*TTY* stands for *teletypewriter*, a telecommunications device used by the audibly impaired to translate spoken words into text.)

2

Setup, Sync, and Settings

If you've read Chapter 1, you're familiar with the layout of your iPhone and iPod touch and how to interact with them. What say you now make them more useful and pleasurable devices by adding some music, movies, contacts, and events, and configuring the devices so you can send and receive email?

Setup

It's time to establish a relationship between the device and iTunes to make it comfortable with your media, email accounts, and personal information.

Get iTunes

iTunes is, in nearly all instances, the conduit for passing information between your computer and the iPhone and iPod touch. Without it, your device will be a pretty limited hunk of technology. Therefore, if you don't have a copy of iTunes 10 or later, now's the time to make a beeline for www.apple.com/itunes/download. Any iPhone or iPod touch running the iOS 4 or iOS 5 software can't be synced without this version (or later) of iTunes, and Apple doesn't include it—or any other software—in the box your device came in.

iTunes is available in both Macintosh and Windows versions. For the device to work with your Mac, you must be running Mac OS X 10.5.8 on a Mac with a USB 2.0 port. PC users must be running Windows XP (with Service Pack 3 or later), Vista, or Windows 7 on a PC with a USB 2.0 port.

Configure the device

In the deep, dark past (OK, as recently as mid-2011), you had to physically attach your iPhone or iPod touch to your computer before you could do anything with it. That's changed. Thanks to iOS 5, you can start configuring your device as soon as you pull it from the box, provided that you have a Wi-Fi network you can connect your device to (such as the one in the Apple Store).

Just press and hold the Sleep/Wake button on the top of the device, and you'll see a gray welcome screen with the name of the device on it: iPhone or iPod touch. Slide the arrow slider at the bottom of the screen to the right to continue. You'll see a series of screens that give you the option to do all the following things:

- Select a language.

- Choose a country or region.

- Turn Location Services on or off. (Location Services allows your device to share its location with apps and services such as Find My iPhone/iPod.)

- Choose a Wi-Fi network. (You can choose to connect to iTunes at this point if you're not within range of an open Wi-Fi network.) If you have an iPhone, wait for it to be activated.

- Set up the device as a new iPhone or iPod touch, restore it from an iCloud backup, or restore it from an iTunes backup (**Figure 2.1**).

Figure 2.1
You can choose to set your device up as new or restore from a backup when you initially set up the iPhone or iPod touch.

- Sign in with an Apple ID.

- Agree to Apple's terms and conditions.

- Sign into an iCloud account, and choose whether to back up your device's data via iCloud or iTunes.

- Enable Siri (iPhone 4S only).

- Enable Find My iPhone/iPod. (This iCloud feature allows you to track your device's location with a Web browser or other iOS device, so no iCloud, no Find My iPhone/iPod.)

- Allow (or not) your device to send Apple diagnostic information. (This information could include data that tells Apple which cell towers your device has been in contact with.)

Phew. That sounds like a lot to go through, but honestly, it grants you access to your device more quickly than at any time in the past, and it takes care of many of the settings that you'd normally have to muck around with in iTunes or on the device itself. When you're ready to begin using your iPhone or iPod touch, just tap the Start Using button at the bottom of the last screen, and you're ready to do something with it.

If you don't have access to a Wi-Fi network, you can attach your device to your computer and configure it the old-fashioned way. Truth be told, if you want to restore your iPod touch or iPhone from a backup on your computer, you'll still have to plug it into your computer, even if you've performed the initial setup over Wi-Fi. What you see when you plug in your device depends on whether and how you initially configured it. If you've chosen to sync your data by using Apple's iCloud service, when you select your device in iTunes, you'll see a Set Up Your iPhone/iPod screen (**Figure 2.2**) with a Name field that contains your name followed by the word *iPhone* or *iPod—Chris Breen's iPhone,* for example. A message follows, indicating that you're using iCloud to sync your calendars, contacts, bookmarks, and notes. Below this message is a checked Automatically Sync Applications option. Click Continue, and if this option is enabled, iTunes will sync all your apps to the device. If you've disabled this option, you can later choose which apps you'd like to sync.

Figure 2.2
The setup screen for a new device within iTunes.

If you haven't chosen to restore your device from an iTunes backup on your computer, you'll be prompted to connect it to that computer. When you do, iTunes should launch automatically (launch it yourself if it doesn't), and you'll see a different version of the Set Up Your iPhone/iPod screen. On this screen, you have the option to set up your iPhone or iPod touch as a new device or restore it from a backup if you previously used an iPhone or iPod touch with this computer.

To restore your iPhone or iPod touch with old information, simply select the Restore from the Backup Of *x* radio button, click the pop-up menu to the right, choose the backup you'd like to restore from (the Last Synced entry below the menu tells you the age of this backup), and then click Continue. The device displays *Restore in Progress* while iTunes restores it with the data from the backup you selected.

> **tip** Alternatively, you can right-click (Control-click on the Mac) the device's icon in iTunes' Source list and choose Restore from Backup from the resulting contextual menu. In the window that appears, use the pop-up menu to choose the backup you'd like to use.

If this iPhone or iPod touch is your first iOS device, you'll see a Name field containing something like *Joe Blow's iPod* and, below that, the Automatically Sync Contacts, Calendars, Bookmarks, Notes, and Email Accounts option. (I discuss this option shortly.)

If you're using a Mac, iTunes syncs the iPhone or iPod touch with your Address Book contacts, Yahoo Address Book contacts, Google Contacts, iCal calendars, Safari bookmarks, and Apple Mail accounts.

If you're using a Windows PC, iTunes syncs contacts from Yahoo Address Book, Windows Address Book (called Windows Contacts in Windows Vista and Windows 7), Google Contacts, or Microsoft Outlook; calendars from Outlook; and email accounts from Windows Mail (included with Vista), Outlook Express (Windows XP), or Outlook.

Notes are synced to Apple's Mail on a Mac and to Outlook on a PC.

Below this option is Automatically Sync Apps. Again, if this device is your first iOS device, you probably don't have many (or any) apps to sync. If you'd rather tell iTunes exactly what information to sync, you can do this later and in a more specific fashion. To choose the manual method, simply clear the Automatically Sync options in this window and then click Done.

If you chose to sync to iTunes halfway through the setup process on the device, you're not entirely done. When the iPhone or iPod touch is restored, the device will ask you to complete a few more steps, including enabling Location Services, connecting to a Wi-Fi network (if possible), signing in with your Apple ID, agreeing to Apple's license, and choosing whether to send diagnostic information to Apple.

Meet iCloud

I've been throwing this iCloud thing around loosely enough that by this point, you'd probably like to know more about what it is. Wait no longer.

What is iCloud?

iCloud is the single name given to a collection of services launched by Apple in October 2011. With an iCloud account, you'll find it much easier to sync your data among your computer, your device, and the Internet. All the iCloud services except iTunes Match are free. Those services include

- **Data synchronization.** Within the iCloud screen (which you access from the Mail, Contacts, Calendars screen), you can switch on separate options for synchronizing mail, contacts, calendars, reminders, bookmarks, and notes. When you enable these options, this information is coordinated among devices so that each device has the latest data. When you add a calendar event to an iCloud calendar, for example, any other device that you use with an iCloud account—another iOS device or your computer—is updated with that event.

- **Data storage.** This service includes optional backups of your email, the Photo app's Camera Roll, documents, device settings, app data, Home-screen and app organization, messages, and ringtones.

- **Photo Stream.** Switch this feature on, and when you take a picture or movie with your iPhone or iPod touch, it's uploaded to the iCloud service and then downloaded (and likewise configured to your Photo Stream) to your other devices when they're connected to a Wi-Fi network. Find out more about Photo Stream in Chapter 8.

- **Find My iPhone/iPod.** The iPhone and iPod touch know where they are, thanks to their location capabilities. If you switch on Find My iPhone/iPod in the iCloud screen, you can track it down later via the Web. I discuss Find My iPhone/iPod in greater detail in Chapter 10.

- **iTunes in the Cloud.** When you activate this feature (it's also known as Automatic Downloads and can be configured within the Store setting in the Settings app), music, apps, or e-books that you purchase from one of Apple's electronic stores download to all your iOS devices automatically. Additionally, you can download past music or TV-show purchases from the iTunes Store without having to pay for that content again. I discuss iTunes in the Cloud in Chapter 6.

- **iTunes Match.** Whereas the free iTunes in the Cloud service lets you download music, TV shows, and books that you've purchased from Apple's stores, the $25-per-year iTunes Match service allows you to upload tracks that you haven't purchased from the iTunes Store to Apple's servers for later retrieval. I also discuss iTunes Match in Chapter 6.

- **Documents in the Cloud.** This service keeps your compatible documents synchronized, like so: Suppose that you have a copy of Apple's Pages word processing app on both your iPod touch and iPhone. When you update a document on your iPod touch, those changes are also delivered to your iPhone.

iCloud setup

Now that you know what iCloud is, set it up as follows:

1. On your iPhone or iPod touch, tap Settings > iCloud.

2. In the next screen, enter your Apple ID and password in the correct fields.

   If you don't have an Apple ID, tap the Get a Free Apple ID button at the bottom of the window and walk through the process of obtaining that Apple ID; then enter your ID and password.

3. Tap Sign In.

4. In the resulting iCloud screen, choose the content you want to sync with iCloud—mail, contacts, calendars, reminders, bookmarks, and/or notes.

5. Do one of the following things on your computer:

- **Macintosh** (running Mac OS X Lion 10.7 or later): Launch System Preferences, click the iCloud preference, sign in to your iCloud account, and choose the data you want to sync from your computer to iCloud.

- **Windows PC** (running Windows Vista or Windows 7): Download and install the iCloud Control Panel from www.icloud.com/icloudcontrolpanel. Then choose Control Panel > Network and Internet > iCloud. As on the Mac, choose the items you want to sync: mail, contacts, calendars, tasks, and/or bookmarks.

 iCloud is compatible with Outlook 2007 and 2010, Safari 5.1.1, and Internet Explorer 8 and later.

That's it. iCloud is ready to sync data among your computer, the cloud, and your iPhone or iPod touch.

Tabtastic

If you've synced an iPod with your Mac or PC lately, you won't be startled by the iPhone or iPod touch Preferences window in iTunes. Like a regular iPod's Preferences window, this one contains a series of tabs for syncing data to the device. Those tabs shake out as follows.

Summary

As its name suggests, the Summary tab (**Figure 2.3**) provides an overview of your device. Here, you find the iPod's or iPhone's name (which you can change by clicking it in iTunes' Source list and entering a new name), its capacity, the software version it's running, its serial number, and (if it's an iPhone) its phone number.

Figure 2.3
*An iPhone's
Summary tab.*

tip Should anyone ask you for the device's UDID (Unique Device Identity), you can find that information by clicking the Serial Number entry.

In the Version section of the tab, you learn whether your device's software is up to date. You can make sure that you have the latest version by clicking the Check for Update button. Here, you also find a Restore button for placing a new version of the iOS software on the device.

The Backup area is new with iOS 5. Here, you see options for backing up your data to iCloud (an iCloud account is required) or to your computer. When you choose to back up to iCloud, all your device's data is stored in the cloud—that is, on Apple's servers via the Internet. If you choose Back up to This Computer instead, your data is backed up exactly there—on your computer. When you select this second option, you have the additional option of encrypting the backup.

When you check Encrypt iPhone/iPod Backup, you ask iTunes to back up your device and password-protect your data. You might do this on an iPhone or iPod touch containing sensitive financial or personal information that you back up to your computer.

When you select this option, you'll be prompted to enter and verify a password. Thereafter, your device will be backed up completely (even if you just backed it up recently), and the backup will be protected. Should you want to change the password—say, because foreign agents weaseled it out of you with promises of clandestine smooches—click the Change Password button, enter your old password, and then enter and verify a new password.

note Encrypting a backup can take iTunes a very long time, so this is another before-you-go-to-bed option. Unless you suffer from insomnia, the job should be complete when you wake up.

The Summary tab displays six check-box options when you plug an iPhone or iPod touch into your computer:

Open iTunes When This iPhone/iPod Is Connected. The first option does that and a bit more: It tells iTunes to launch whenever you dock the iPhone or iPod touch and then to sync the device. Disable this option if you prefer to launch iTunes yourself and start syncing the device manually or if you've chosen to sync it over Wi-Fi. This setting is carried with the device, which means that regardless of which computer you jack the iPhone or iPod touch into, it does what this setting instructs.

tip The Devices panel of the iTunes Preferences window contains an option that lets you modify this behavior: the Prevent iPods, iPhones, and iPads from Syncing Automatically check box. The option in the Summary tab applies only to an individual device; the iTunes setting applies to all iOS devices. When you check this box, iTunes will still launch if you have the Open iTunes When This iPhone/iPod Is Connected option enabled, but iTunes won't sync your device automatically.

Sync With This iPhone/iPod over Wi-Fi. Again, the iPhone and iPod touch can sync now without the need for a cable. To enable this option, you have to first attach your device to your computer with the sync cable, select it in iTunes' Source list, enable this option, and click the Apply button in the bottom-right corner of the iTunes window. Thereafter, you can disconnect the device and sync it over Wi-Fi as long as your computer and device are on the same Wi-Fi network and the iPhone or iPod touch is connected to a power source. I discuss how to activate Wi-Fi syncing on the device itself later in this chapter.

Sync Only Checked Songs and Videos. The third option tells the device to sync only those items that you've selected in your iTunes Library. If you want greater control of what's planted on your iPhone or iPod touch, you can select some songs or videos in a playlist in your iTunes Library, but not others. The check boxes appear next to the names of the items— *Stacey's Mom* and *The Graduate*, for example. When this option is turned on, whenever you sync the device, it syncs only the items you've checked.

Prefer Standard Definition Videos. The fourth option is a space-saving option that appears only when you plug a 4G iPod touch (or later) or iPhone 4 (or later) into your computer. (This option is absent on iPod touches and iPhones that lack a retina display.) When you purchase or rent high-definition (HD) videos from iTunes on one of these late-model devices, the iTunes Store provides two versions—standard definition (SD) and high definition—and you can sync either version to your iPhone or iPod touch. HD videos looks great, but they take up a lot of space. When you enable this option, iTunes will sync the SD version of a video rather than the HD version.

Convert Higher Bit Rate Songs to 128 Kbps AAC. The next option is another space-saving measure. The higher a song's bit rate is, the better it sounds, but the more space it consumes. The iTunes Store sells songs encoded at 256 Kbps, which is twice the bit rate and twice the size of a 128 Kbps version. If you want to pack as much music as possible on your device, you may want to enable this option.

> **tip** iTunes performs the conversion to 128 Kbps AAC as it syncs files, but it doesn't keep copies of these lower-bit-rate tracks on your computer, so you needn't worry about your hard drive being eaten up with redundant songs. This process adds quite a bit of time to the syncing process, which isn't a big deal if you sync your media the night before you need it, but if you're in a hurry, switch this option off.

Manually Manage Music and Videos. This last option makes it possible to drag content from your iTunes Library to the iPhone or iPod touch in iTunes' Source list when you've physically connected the device to iTunes. You can't do this to add music from another computer's library; the iPhone or iPod touch can be synced with only one iTunes Library.

> **tip** This option is a good one to use when you want to add something to the device quickly, without going through the whole syncing rigmarole.

At the very bottom of the tab, you'll also see a Configure Universal Access button. Click it to open a Universal Access dialog box, where you can choose which (if any) of the device's accessibility features to switch on (**Figure 2.4**).

Figure 2.4
iTunes' Universal Access dialog box.

Down Below

I would be remiss if I left the Summary tab without mentioning the Capacity bar at the bottom (**Figure 2.5**). This bar details how your device's storage space is being used. Here, you view the total capacity of your iPhone or iPod touch, along with statistics for Audio, Video, Photos, Apps, Books, Other (a category that includes contacts and calendars, for example), and Free (as in free space).

Figure 2.5
The iTunes Capacity bar.

(Continues on next page)

Down Below (continued)

By default, the amount of storage consumed by a particular item appears below its heading (*Video 1.45 GB*, for example). But if you click one of the entries below the Capacity bar, the statistics labels change—first to the number of items in each category and then, with another click, to the amount of time it would take to play all the videos and audio stored on the device (*2.5 days*, for example).

When you choose media to sync with your iPod touch or iPhone, the Capacity bar changes to reflect how the device's storage will be allocated after you sync the device. If you've chosen more media than will fit, an Over Capacity warning appears at the end of the bar.

To the right of the Capacity bar are one or two buttons. If you've made any changes. you'll see both a Revert and Apply button. Clicking Revert puts the settings back the way they were before you started mucking around with them. Click Apply, and the changes will be applied. At this point, you see a single Sync button in this space. Click it, and iTunes syncs your device using the selected settings.

Info

The Info tab (**Figure 2.6**) is where you choose which data—contacts, calendars, mail accounts, browser bookmarks, and notes—you'd like to sync to your device.

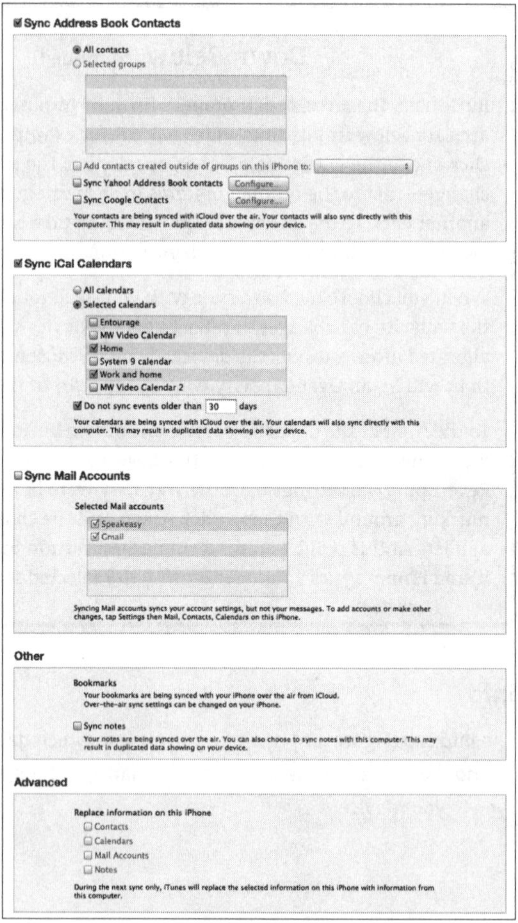

Figure 2.6
The Info tab.

☑ **Sync Address Book Contacts**

- ● All contacts
- ○ Selected groups

☐ Add contacts created outside of groups on this iPhone to: [　　　　　　▼]
☐ Sync Yahoo! Address Book contacts [Configure]
☐ Sync Google Contacts [Configure...]

Your contacts are being synced with iCloud over the air. Your contacts will also sync directly with this computer. This may result in duplicated data showing on your device.

☑ **Sync iCal Calendars**

- ○ All calendars
- ● Selected calendars
  - ☐ Entourage
  - ☐ MW Video Calendar
  - ☑ Home
  - ☐ System 9 calendar
  - ☑ Work and home
  - ☐ MW Video Calendar 2

☑ Do not sync events older than [30] days

Your calendars are being synced with iCloud over the air. Your calendars will also sync directly with this computer. This may result in duplicated data showing on your device.

☐ **Sync Mail Accounts**

Selected Mail accounts
- ☑ Speakeasy
- ☑ Gmail

Syncing Mail accounts syncs your account settings, but not your messages. To add accounts or make other changes, tap Settings then Mail, Contacts, Calendars on this iPhone.

Other

Bookmarks
Your bookmarks are being synced with your iPhone over the air from iCloud.
Over-the-air sync settings can be changed on your iPhone.

☐ Sync notes
Your notes are being synced over the air. You can also choose to sync notes with this computer. This may result in duplicated data showing on your device.

Advanced

Replace information on this iPhone
- ☐ Contacts
- ☐ Calendars
- ☐ Mail Accounts
- ☐ Notes

During the next sync only, iTunes will replace the selected information on this iPhone with information from this computer.

Sync Address Book Contacts

Here, you find settings for syncing all your contacts or just selected groups that you've created in Address Book (if you use a Mac) or in Windows Address Book, Outlook, Yahoo Address Book, and Google Contacts. (On a Mac, the Yahoo and Google options are listed at the bottom of the Contacts area. Click the Configure button next to either one, agree to the license agreement, and enter your Yahoo or Google user name and password. When this option is enabled, your Yahoo Address Book and Google contacts will make their way to the device too.)

You also find an option for automatically adding contacts to a specific group—a Strangers group, for example—if you don't assign a contact that you've created to another group.

Sync iCal Calendars

This area works similarly. You can choose to sync all your calendars or, if you're using a Mac, just selected calendars that you've created in Apple's iCal—your work calendar, for example, but not your personal calendar. (I discuss calendars in depth in Chapter 4.)

You also have the option to not sync events older than a certain number of days. Calendar data takes up very little room on your device, but if you're tidy or don't care to carry that incriminating "Meet Becky for Pillow Fight" appointment from last April around with you, enable this option, and enter an appropriate number of days.

Sync Mail Accounts

iTunes looks for email account settings in Mail on a Mac and in Outlook, Microsoft Mail, and Outlook Express on a Windows PC. (It looks for the settings only; syncing mail accounts doesn't sync messages.) The settings that it finds appear in a list in the Sync Mail Accounts section of the Info tab. You have the option to select the email account(s) you'd like to access with the iPhone or iPod touch.

Other

In this area of the Info tab, you find two settings: one for syncing browser bookmarks and the other for syncing notes. In the Macintosh version of iTunes, you have a single Sync Safari Bookmarks option. On a Windows PC, a pop-up menu provides the option to sync Safari or Internet Explorer bookmarks. Sync Notes is an On/Off option. Enable Sync Notes in the Mac version of iTunes, and any notes created on the iPhone or iPod touch will be synced to the Notes area of Mail—Apple's email client. Likewise, if you create a note in Mail and have this option enabled, that note will be synced to your device. On a Windows PC, notes are synced to Outlook (and vice versa here, too). I take a closer look at Notes in Chapter 9.

Advanced

Finally, the Advanced section offers a nifty little workaround when you plug your device into another computer. For this feature to work, you must first choose at least one option above—say, Sync Address Book Contacts—and then choose the options you want in that section (choose to sync a specific group of contacts, for example). Now enable the related option in the Advanced section (you'd choose Contacts if you enabled Sync Address Book Contacts). When you click the Apply button in the bottom-right corner of the tab, iTunes overwrites the selected information that's currently on the device with the information stored on the computer to which the iPhone or iPod touch is connected.

Apps

Your iPhone and iPod touch can use iOS applications (known as *apps* on iOS devices) sold in Apple's App Store. The Apps tab (**Figure 2.7**) is where you manage which of those apps are synced to your device, configure

how apps are arranged on the iPhone's or iPod touch's Home screen,
and transfer documents to and from the device. I look at the App Store
in greater detail in Chapter 7, but if you'd like to take a look now, here's
what you're looking at: All apps that you download from the App Store
(either from within iTunes or from an iPod touch or iPhone) are listed in
this tab. Those apps that you downloaded from an iPod touch or iPhone
are moved to iTunes only when you sync.

Figure 2.7
*The Apps tab in
iTunes.*

The list that appears below the Sync Apps heading contains all the
apps in your iTunes Library. You can sort those apps by name, kind (apps
that work on all iOS devices versus those intended just for the iPhone or
iPod touch, for example), category (Games, for example), date, and size.
You can also use the Search field to search for a particular app. If you
want to sync an app to your device, just check the box next to its name.
At the bottom of this list is an Automatically Sync New Apps check box.
Check it, and any new apps you've downloaded will be placed on your
iPod touch or iPhone the next time you sync it.

tip You can quickly enable or disable all your apps by holding down the Command key (Mac) or Ctrl key (Windows PC) and clicking a check box.

The pane to the right of the apps list displays the various pages of your device's Home screen. Using this pane, you can click and drag icons around to rearrange them. Other icons shift out of the way as you drag. You can even drag icons into and out of the Dock at the bottom of the screen. (You must drag an icon out of the Dock before you can put another one in it.) And just as you can on the device (as I describe in Chapter 1), you can create folders by dragging icons on top of one another. To move an icon from one page to another, just click the page on which the icon resides and drag it to another page in the pane.

The File Sharing section is where you transfer documents to and from the device. If you've downloaded DataViz's Documents To Go app—an app that lets you open and edit many Microsoft Office files—you can select DocsToGo in the Apps list and then drag a Microsoft Word file to the adjacent DocsToGo documents list. The file will transfer to the device immediately; you don't have to sync it for this to happen. If you'd like to transfer a document that you created in Documents To Go from your iPhone or iPod touch to your computer, just select DocsToGo in the Apps list and then drag the document from the documents list to your computer's desktop. (If you're a traditionalist who objects to all this newfangled dragging, you can also employ the Add and Save To buttons at the bottom of the documents list to transfer documents to and from the device, respectively.)

Ringtones

Both the iPhone and iPod touch can play ringtones that you purchase from the iTunes Store or create in an application such as Apple's GarageBand. In the Ringtones tab, you choose which ringtones to sync with your device—all or just selected ringtones.

Music

The Music tab (**Figure 2.8**) is one gateway to syncing music to your iPhone or iPod touch. If you've subscribed to iTunes Match (which I describe in Chapter 6), you don't sync your music via iTunes but grab it from iTunes Match. Enable the Sync Music option and then choose to sync your entire music library or just selected playlists, artists, albums, and genres. When you enable the Selected Playlists, Artists, Albums, and Genres option, four lists appear below it: Playlists, Artists, Genres, and Albums. To choose music to sync to the device, just enable the check boxes next to the playlists, artists, genres, and/or albums you want to transfer. In Chapter 6, I discuss how to sync music most efficiently.

Figure 2.8
The Music tab.

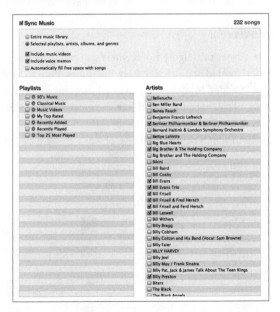

note You don't have the option to copy specific songs to your device unless you choose Manually Manage Music and Videos in the Summary tab. Do that, and you can drag any music you like to the iPhone or iPod touch to add it. If you enable the Sync Music option in this tab, however, the only way to add specific songs is to create a playlist that contains that music and then sync the playlist to the device.

Here, you also find options for including music videos and voice memos (audible notes that you've recorded with the Voice Memos app, which I discuss in Chapter 9). Additionally, you can enable an Automatically Fill Free Space with Songs option. If your iPhone or iPod touch has remaining storage space after it's synced the data and media you've asked it to, and if this option is enabled, it tops off the device with tunes.

Movies

The Movies tab (**Figure 2.9**) is where you configure the transfer of movies you've rented or purchased from the iTunes Store, as well as other movies you've added to your iTunes Library. I cover movie rentals in Chapter 7. For now, all you need to know is that the movies you rent from the iTunes Store appear in the top portion of this tab. From there, you can transfer them to your iPod touch, iPhone, or video-capable click-wheel iPod.

Figure 2.9
The Movies tab.

You have a few options in this tab as well. Enable the Sync Movies option, and in the area just below it, you have the choice to automatically add all the movies in your iTunes Library (an option you should select only if you have very few movies or many very short movies); the 1, 3, 5, or 10 most recently added movies; all unwatched movies; 1, 3, 5, or 10 most recent unwatched movies; or 1, 3, 5, or 10 least recent unwatched movies.

You can skip automatic syncing by disabling this option. At that point, a list of all the compatible movies in your iTunes Library appears. Just tick the check boxes next to those movies that you want to sync to the device. Additionally, you can sync playlists of movies to your iPhone or iPod touch. To do that, turn your attention to the Include Movies from Playlists section at the bottom of the tab, and check the boxes next to the playlists you want to sync.

TV Shows

The TV Shows tab works very similarly to the Movies tab. The main difference is that you can select episodes of particular shows to sync to your device. Clear the Automatically Include check box, and a list of shows appears in the appropriately named Shows list. Select a show you want to sync, and its available episodes appear in the Episodes list to the right. Episodes in this list are broken down by season, making it easier to identify just the episodes you want. Check the box next to the season entry—Season 2, for example—and you can sync all the available episodes from that season. Alternatively, you can select individual episodes.

Podcasts

You can listen to podcasts on your iPhone or iPod touch. Because people tend to listen to lots of podcasts, some of which tend to be long (their files therefore taking up significant amounts of room), the Podcasts tab lets you manage which ones are synced to your device.

As in each one of these tabs, you have the option to not sync this content, but if you choose to do so, you have plenty of options. Rather than repeat myself, I'll just say that you'll find lots of options for syncing new unplayed, recent unplayed, and least recent unplayed podcast episodes. As with TV shows, you can select particular podcasts in the Podcasts list and choose just the episodes you want to play in the Episodes list to the right. And of course, you can sync playlists of podcasts, just as you can playlists of movies and TV shows.

> **tip** Both video and audio podcasts are listed in this tab. Because video can consume a lot of storage space, be careful how you choose your video podcasts.

For more on podcasts, check Chapter 6.

iTunes U

iTunes U provides audio and video content from such providers as universities, American Public Media, the Library of Congress, and the Metropolitan Museum of Art. And it's all *free!* Download some of this content via the iTunes U tab, and you'll see that it can be synced very much like podcasts.

Books

With iOS 4, iPhones and iPod touches support *e-books*—electronic books that can be read on computers; dedicated e-book readers; and iOS devices. iTunes' Books tab (**Figure 2.10**) is where you choose the e-books, PDF files, and audiobooks that you'd like to sync to your device. You can choose to sync all the books in your iTunes Library or just selected titles, and you have the option to view both books and PDF files, only books, and only PDFs, as well as the option to sort books by title or author.

Figure 2.10
The Books tab.

At the bottom of this tab, you find the Sync Audiobooks section. If you choose to sync just selected audiobooks, you have the option to select specific portions of a selected audiobook—the third part, for example, if you've already listened to parts one and two. I cover the ways and means of obtaining books on the device in Chapter 7.

Photos

The Mac and Windows versions of the Photos tab differ slightly. If you use a Mac, the iPhone or iPod touch can sync photos with Apple's iPhoto and Aperture, as well as with your Pictures folder or a different folder of your choosing, as you see in the Mac's Photos tab (**Figure 2.11**). With that Mac, you can additionally sync albums, events, and faces. On a Windows PC, you can sync with your My Pictures folder (called simply Pictures in Vista and Windows 7), a different folder of your choosing, or photo albums created with Adobe Photoshop Elements 3.0 or later or Adobe Photoshop Album 2.0 or later.

Figure 2.11
The Photos tab on a Macintosh.

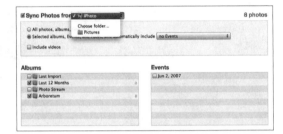

Settings

Although you'll control much of your iPhone's or iPod touch's behavior within its apps, some global settings have some bearing on how it performs. You access the Settings screen (**Figure 2.12**) by tapping the Settings icon on the device's Home screen. As you might expect, the iPhone's and iPod touch's Settings screens differ slightly because the iPhone offers some phonecentric features that aren't available on the iPod touch. Here's what their screens contain.

Figure 2.12
An iPhone's Settings screen.

Airplane Mode

As you're now aware, the iPhone and iPod touch are wireless communications devices, and wireless communications can interfere with an
aircraft's navigation system. Thus, the aptly named Airplane Mode option
lets you switch off features that take advantage of the devices' Wi-Fi
and Bluetooth talents (email, Web browsing, messaging, and Location
Services, for example), as well as telephone talents (in the case of the
iPhone), but still use the devices' other features.

This mode is a simple On/Off setting. When you turn it on, the device
disables its wireless functions.

Wi-Fi

The iPhone and iPod touch support 802.11 wireless networking. In this
screen, you can turn Wi-Fi on or off. Turning it off saves some battery
power. I describe the workings of the devices' Wi-Fi settings in the
"Network" section later in this chapter.

Notifications

With iOS 5, Apple has expanded the capabilities of notations in a significant way. The most obvious way is Notification Center, a gray screen that
you can access from anywhere on the device simply by dragging down
your finger from the menu bar at the top of the screen. (This also works
when you're working with an app in landscape mode.) When you first set
up your iPhone or iPod touch, that screen will likely contain just weather
and stocks information. But other apps are supported as well, including
Phone (iPhone only), FaceTime (iPod touch only), Messages, Reminders,
Calendar, and Game Center. Third-party applications configured to
support notifications may appear too.

When you tap the Notifications entry in the Settings screen, you're taken to the Notifications screen, where you can configure the behavior of Notification Center. The first entry, Sort Apps, allows you to sort notifications manually (you can choose their positions) or by time (the most recent notifications appear at the top of the list). To change the position of an app in Notification Center, tap Manually, tap the Edit button in the screen's top-right corner, and use the drag bars next to the apps below to move them up or down the list of apps. Click Done when you're finished.

Speaking of those apps, below the Sort Apps area is the In Notification Center area. Here, you'll see a list of any apps currently configured to use Notification Center. Below the name of each application, you see which notifications are enabled for it—badges, alerts, and banners, for example. Tap an app, and you're taken to its specific Notifications screen (**Figure 2.13**), where you can choose to turn it off so that it no longer appears in Notification Center; choose the number of notifications that app can display (1, 5, or 10 items); and select an alert style (none, banners, or alerts). For some apps, you can additionally choose an On or Off setting for displaying badge icons (small red numbers that appear on an icon when a new event or action is added) and for viewing the app's notifications on the lock screen. The Messages app additionally includes options for showing a message preview and repeating an alert (your choices are never, once, twice, three times, five times, and ten times).

tip What's the difference between an alert and a banner? An *alert* is a window that requires some action from you for it to go away—tap Accept, for example. A *banner* appears as a short string of text (preceded by an app's icon) that appears for a few seconds at the top of your device's screen before disappearing. You can view these alerts by swiping the screen down to expose Notification Center.

Figure 2.13
Notification settings for the Phone app.

If you switch off notifications for a particular app, the app's name appears at the bottom of the Notifications screen below the Not in Notification Center heading. Should you want to make it rejoin your other notifications, simply tap it and slide the Notification Center switch to On.

Location Services

iOS devices have ways of determining their location. iPhones use GPS circuitry, cell-tower triangulation, and Wi-Fi networks. iPod touches rely on Wi-Fi networks, as they don't have GPS or phone circuitry. The Location Services screen (**Figure 2.14**) lets you determine how (or whether) location works on your device. To switch off location entirely, simply flip the Location Services switch off. Your iPhone or iPod touch will stop tracking its location.

Figure 2.14
*An iPhone's
Location Services
screen.*

Below the switch is an area where you can turn off Location Services for specific apps—Weather or Twitter, for example. You may also see a small arrow next to an app. A purple arrow indicates an app that is currently using Location Services; a gray arrow marks an app that has used location in the past 24 hours.

At the bottom of this screen is a System Services button. Tap it to see how your device is using location systemwide. On an iPod touch, you have the option to switch off two settings: Location-Based Ads (advertisements served by Apple based on where you are) and Setting Time Zone (for automatically keeping your device's clock in sync with the local time).

The iPhone, with its cellular capabilities, has additional options, including Call Network Search, Compass Calibration, Diagnostics & Usage, and Traffic. Of these, the only one I can image that anyone would find objectionable is Diagnostics & Usage. Apple uses this information to track cell-tower strength. It keeps a very, *very* general record of where you've traveled with your device. If you prefer to not share that information with Apple, turn this option off.

Finally, at the bottom of this screen for both devices, you find a Status Bar Icon On/Off switch. When this switch is on, you'll see a small purple arrow in the status bar whenever the app you're working in is using Location Services.

Sounds

The appearance of the Sounds screen (**Figure 2.15**) is marginally different on the iPhone and iPod touch. At the top of the screen on an iPhone, you see a Vibrate entry below the Silent heading. If you want your iPhone to vibrate when you've set the phone's side switch to Silent, switch this on. The iPod touch doesn't have such a side switch, so this entry isn't necessary.

Figure 2.15
The Sounds screen on an iPhone.

At the top of the iPod touch's Sounds screen and below the Silent entry on the iPhone's screen, you see a volume slider. This slider adjusts the volume of the device's ringer (used by the iPhone's phone features and for FaceTime on an iPod touch) and alerts. Below this slider is a Change with Buttons option. Turn it on, and you can use the device's volume buttons to adjust the loudness of the ringer and alerts. Below the slider, you see a list of actions (Text Tone and New Mail, for example). Tap an action, and in the succeeding screen, you can assign an alert sound or ringtone to that action.

At the bottom of the Sounds screen are options for turning on or off lock sounds and keyboard clicks—the sounds that the iPhone or iPod touch makes when you type with its virtual keyboard.

Brightness

By default, the iPhone and iPod touch adjust their displays automatically, based on the light they sense around them. When you're outdoors on a sunny day, for example, the screen brightens; when you're inside a dark room, the display dims. If you'd like to override the automatic brightness settings—when you want to save battery power by making the display dimmer than the device thinks necessary, for example—you do so in this screen. Switch the Auto-Brightness option off and drag the slider to adjust brightness up or down.

Wallpaper

On the iPhone and iPod touch, *wallpaper* refers to an image you choose as a background for the Home screen—an image that also appears when you unlock the device. To set and adjust your wallpaper picture, tap the Wallpaper control and then navigate to an image file in the collection provided by Apple (listed below the Wallpaper heading), pictures you've taken with the device's camera, or images you've synced to the iPhone or iPod touch. Just tap the image you want to use, and you see a preview of it as wallpaper (**Figure 2.16**).

Figure 2.16
Choosing wallpaper.

You can move any of your images by dragging them around or enlarge them by using the stretch gesture (see Chapter 1). When you're happy with the picture's orientation, tap Set. A sheet rolls up from the bottom of the screen, listing four options: Set Lock Screen, Set Home Screen, Set Both, and Cancel. Tap any but the last one to set your wallpaper.

Interestingly enough, you can't resize any of the images that Apple includes in its Wallpaper collection (because, one assumes, they're perfect just as they are).

General

The General settings are...well, pretty general. The grouping consists of a hodgepodge of controls (**Figure 2.17**). I'll point out where there are differences between the two devices.

Figure 2.17

*The iPhone's
General settings
screen.*

About

This screen provides your device's vital statistics. The iPhone displays
a few more entries than the iPod touch—the network it's using, the
version number of the firmware used by the phone's modem, and some
identification numbers. On each device, you find information regarding
the number of audio tracks, videos, photos, and apps on the device; total
capacity; how much storage space remains; software version; serial and
model numbers; Wi-Fi and Bluetooth addresses; and Legal and Regulatory
commands that, when tapped, lead to a seemingly endless screen of legal
mumbo jumbo and various associations' signatory badges, respectively.

New with iOS 5 is a Diagnostics & Usage entry. Tap it, and you can choose to send (or not send) usage information about your device to Apple. (This data can include some location information.).You can also tap a Diagnostic & Usage Data button and then, on the resulting screen, tap a particular report to see the contents of certain preferences files and error messages. This feature is helpful when troubleshooting a misbehaving device, as I discuss in Chapter 10.

Software Update

Among iOS 5's wireless delights is its newfound capability to update an iOS device's software over a Wi-Fi connection. Just tap this entry, and if a new software version is available, you can tap the link to download it. After the download, the latest iOS software is installed on your device.

Usage

If you've ever wondered how your iOS device's resources are being allocated, you can find out within this screen. Below the Storage entry, you see a list of all the device's active apps, accompanied by the amount of storage they currently consume. Tap an entry to learn how much storage is consumed by the app's documents and data. Within one of the app screens, you also find a Delete App button. Tap it if you want to quickly remove an app that's eating up huge amounts of your device's storage.

If you've signed up for an iCloud account, you see usage statistics next, including total storage, available storage, and a Manage Storage entry. Tap this last entry, and you can see the names of the devices being backed up to iCloud.

Tap a device, and the Info screen that appears should show you the time of the latest backup, its size, and a list of the apps whose data will be backed up the next time your device is backed up. You can turn off those apps that you don't want to back up by tapping Delete Backup near the bottom of the screen. (You might tap this button if you're running out of iCloud storage and want to start over with a fresh backup.) The very bottom of the screen includes text and a meter indicating how much storage you've used—*3GB of 5GB on iCloud,* for example.

tip If you find that you need more storage than the 5 GB offered for free, tap the Buy More Storage button on the Manage Storage screen. A sheet appears, offering to sell you 10 GB, 20 GB, or 50 GB of additional storage for $20, $40, or $100 a year, respectively. Choose the option you want, tap Buy, and enter your Apple ID.

The iPhone includes a couple more entries on the Usage screen, the first of which is Battery Percentage. To view the amount of charge you have remaining as a percentage—84%, for example—rather than as an icon, flip this switch to On. The other entry is Cellular Usage. Tap it, and you'll see statistics on your call time and the amount of data you've used on the cellular network. This information is useful if you have a bandwidth limit on your iPhone (as most people do), and you think you're nearing that limit.

Siri (iPhone 4S only)

As you may have read in Chapter 1, Siri is Apple's voice-controlled intelligent assistant. This setting screen is where you configure it.

If you don't want to use Siri, you can turn it off with the On/Off toggle switch at the top of the screen. When you do, the information that Siri has gathered to better understand your life (the contacts you've associated with your boyfriend and sister, for example) is deleted from Apple's servers, but it's still stored on your iPhone. When you switch Siri back on, this information is sent to Apple's servers again. With Siri switched off, when you click and hold the Home button, your iPhone 4S behaves just like an iPhone 4 and 4G iPod touch, presenting the Voice Control screen, where you can command your iPhone to play music or call contacts.

When Siri is switched on, you see these additional options:

- **Language.** Siri speaks English (Australian, UK, and U.S.), French, and German. Tap this option, and you can choose the dialect/language you'd like Siri to speak in.

- **Voice Feedback.** At times, you may prefer that Siri keep quiet—when you're in a library, for example. Tap Voice Feedback and then Handsfree Only, and Siri will vocalize only when you're using a wired headset or Bluetooth audio with your iPhone. (The other option is Always, meaning that Siri will always pipe up when given the opportunity.)

- **My Info.** Tap this option to choose your contact entry from Contacts. Then Siri can use this information when you ask something like "Where do I live?"

- **Raise to Speak.** By default, if you raise your iPhone to your ear, Siri becomes active. If you'd rather invoke Siri by clicking and holding the Home button, turn this option off.

Network

On an iPod touch, the Network settings screen includes only options for configuring virtual private networks (VPN) and Wi-Fi.

VPN is an encrypted network protocol that many companies use because it allows authorized outsiders to join the company network, regardless of their locations. Your IT professional can help you set up VPN.

When you tap the Wi-Fi entry in the Network screen, you're taken to the Wi-Fi Networks screen, atop which appears an On/Off switch for enabling or disabling Wi-Fi on your device (Disabling Wi-Fi conserves power.) Below that switch is the Choose a Network area. Any visible Wi-Fi networks within range appear in a list; those that have a lock icon next to them are password-protected. To access a password-protected network, simply tap its name, enter the password on the keyboard that appears, and tap Join.

To see detailed network information, tap the blue symbol to the right of the network's name. A new screen appears, listing such information as IP Address, Subnet Mask, Router, DNS, Search Domains, and Client ID. At the bottom of one of these screens, you see an HTTP Proxy area, offering the choices Off, Manual, and Auto. Again, an IT or ISP representative will tell you whether you need to muck with these settings.

tip If a network that you never use routinely appears in this list, you can instruct your device to avoid using it by tapping Forget This Network in the resulting screen.

Finally, the bottom of the Wi-Fi Networks screen includes the Ask to Join Networks option. Leave this option switched on (as it is by default), and your iPhone or iPod touch will join known networks automatically and ask to join a network if no known network is available. If you switch the option off, you'll have to join networks manually without being asked. To do so, tap Other; then, using the keyboard that appears, enter the name of the network and password (if required).

The iPhone's Network screen has far more options. They include Enable 3G (On/Off), Cellular Data (On/Off), Data Roaming (On/Off), and Set up Personal Hotspot. They work this way:

- **Enable 3G.** The iPhone is capable of using a carrier's 3G cellular networks, which are faster networks but use more battery power. If you're trying to squeeze every volt out of your battery, consider switching this option off.

- **Cellular Data.** The iPhone can transfer data not only over Wi-Fi, but also over cellular networks. If you turn Cellular Data off, the iPhone will act like an iPod touch and transfer data only when it's attached to a Wi-Fi network. Use this option when you've reached your carrier's monthly cellular data cap.

- **Data Roaming.** This option allows your iPhone to connect to cellular networks outside your home network, such as when you're traveling overseas. This option is here because data roaming can cost a small fortune if you're not careful. I always keep data roaming off to prevent such problems.

- **Set up Personal Hotspot.** As I explain earlier in this list, the iPhone can transfer data over a cellular network, and it can share this cellular network over Wi-Fi. Tap Set up Personal Hotspot, and you'll be given instructions on how to establish this service with your iPhone's carrier. It costs extra; AT&T charges $20 a month for this service as I write this book.

Bluetooth

This setting is a simple On/Off option. When you turn it on, the iPhone or iPod touch becomes discoverable and searches for other Bluetooth devices. Turning Bluetooth off can save power. Any Bluetooth devices you've paired your device with are listed in the Devices area.

To pair a device such as a keyboard with your iPhone or iPod touch, just put it in pairing mode (every device has a different way of doing this); its name should appear on your iPhone's or iPod's screen below the Devices heading. Tap it, and depending on the device (a keyboard, for example), you could be prompted to enter a four-digit code. Do that, and the device should pair with your iPhone or iPod touch, ready to use.

When it's connected, a Bluetooth device displays a blue > icon next to it. Tap this icon, and in the subsequent screen, you see a Forget This Device. Tap it and then tap the resulting confirmation button to unpair the Bluetooth device.

iTunes Wi-Fi Sync

Earlier in this chapter, I mention that iOS devices running iOS 5 and later can sync with iTunes wirelessly. By way of reminder, this feature won't work until you first plug your iPhone or iPod touch into your computer, select it in iTunes' Source list, enable the Sync with This iPhone/iPod over Wi-Fi option in the Summary tab, and click Apply. At this point, your device will sync with iTunes, and you can unplug the device from your computer. It remains in the Source list even though it's not plugged in. Feel free to change its syncing options—sync an additional playlist or add a movie, for example. When you want to update the device, simply click Sync in iTunes or pick up the device, tap Setting > iTunes Wi-Fi Sync, and then tap the Sync Now button.

tip By default, when you've switched Wi-Fi sync on and you plug your iPhone or iPod touch into a power source, it automatically syncs with iTunes, provided that your computer is on and iTunes is running.

Spotlight Search

The iPhone and iPod touch provide several ways to search the contents of your device. The obvious way is to visit the first page of the Home screen and swipe your finger to the right to produce the Search screen. (You can also click the Home button once while you're on the first page of the Home screen to produce the Search screen.)

The power of search goes beyond this screen, however; it's spread throughout the device's apps. When you launch the Contacts app, for example, you'll find a Search field at the top of the screen. This same kind of Search field appears in other apps, including Mail, Notes, and Music. In these apps, however, the Search field doesn't appear by default. To produce it, just tap the device's status menu (where the time is displayed). The Search field bounces down into view.

You can configure what kind of results you get from the main Search screen by tapping the Spotlight Search entry in the General settings screen. In the resulting Spotlight Search screen (**Figure 2.18**), you see a list of items that you can search for on your iPhone or iPod touch. Search results appear in the order in which they're presented in this screen—Contacts, Applications, Music, and so on—but you can change that order by dragging items up or down in the list, using the drag handles on the right side of the screen.

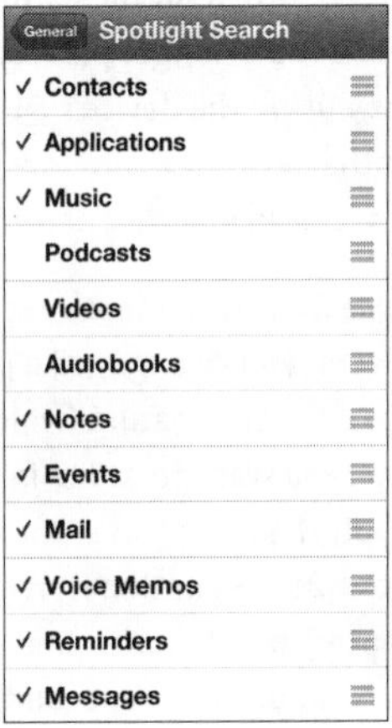

Figure 2.18
Selecting search options.

By default, all these options are enabled. If you don't want certain kinds of items to appear when you search—podcasts and calendar items, for example—just tap them to clear the check marks next to them.

Auto-Lock

The iOS equivalent of a keypad lock, Auto-Lock tells the touchscreen to ignore taps after a customizable period of inactivity. When the device is locked, you can still use its volume buttons (or switch, on earlier iPod touches) to change the volume when listening to music. The button on the optional headset's controller works when the device is locked, too.

Passcode Lock

You can prevent others from viewing the contents of your iPhone or iPod touch by setting a passcode lock. Tap this entry; then enter and verify a four-digit code. If you feel that four digits just don't make your iPhone or iPod touch secure enough, you can switch off the Simple Passcode option. When you do this, you can enter a much longer passcode made up of letters, numbers, and symbols by using the device's QWERTY keyboard. Also, you can choose how long the device remains idle before a passcode is required: immediately; after 1, 5, or 15 minutes; or after 1 or 4 hours.

On an iPhone 4, you'll see a Voice Dial switch that's set to On by default. This setting means that even when you've engaged a passcode lock, anyone can use the phone's Voice Control feature (which allows you to speak the name of the person you want to call to initiate a call; see "International" later in this chapter). Switch this setting off, and the feature is disabled. On the iPhone 4S, this option is named Siri (see the "Siri" section earlier in this chapter), but it works similarly. When the Siri option is switched off, you can't—and, more important, *someone else* can't—use Siri from the lock screen.

On both the iPhone and iPod touch, you'll find the Erase Data option. When this setting is on, if someone fails to enter the correct passcode ten times in a row, the data on the device is erased. To remove your passcode, just tap the Passcode Lock setting in the General settings screen, enter your passcode when prompted, and tap Turn Passcode Off. (This same screen gives you the option to change your passcode.)

Restrictions

You can restrict access to particular apps, as well as clamp down on content synced to the device. To do this, tap Restrictions in the General settings screen. The idea is that a child or otherwise innocent person is going to use the device, and you want to protect him or her from inappropriate content and applications. You do all this within the Restrictions screen (**Figure 2.19**) by restricting not just applications such as Safari, YouTube, Camera, and FaceTime, but also music, movies, and TV shows based on their ratings.

Date & Time

The Date & Time settings include switches for enabling 24-hour time, choosing a time zone, and setting the date and time automatically (using Apple's time servers) or setting it manually by entering the data and time yourself.

Figure 2.19
Restrict and unrestrict the iPhone or iPod touch in this screen.

Keyboard

Care to turn autocapitalization on or off (*on* means that the iPhone or iPod touch automatically capitalizes words after a period, question mark, or exclamation point)? Are you so sensitive about your device's autocorrecting your typing errors that you want to disable that feature? Do you want the iPhone or iPod touch to stop spell-checking your work? Would you like to type in ALL CAPITALS when you double-tap the keyboard's Shift key? And would you like to disable your device's ability to enter a period and space after you double-tap the spacebar? Here's where you do these things.

Below these five On/Off options, you see International Keyboards. Tap it, and you're taken to a Keyboards screen, where you can configure the currently selected keyboard as well as switch on additional keyboards.

The number of activated keyboards is reflected next to the International Keyboard entry in the Keyboard screen—*International Keyboards 5,* for example. You can remove keyboards by navigating to the Keyboards screen, tapping the Edit button, and deleting the keyboards that you no longer need.

iOS 5 introduces a feature that allows you to create text shortcuts. You could create one that, say, expands the shortcut *tgif* to *This gizmo is fantastic!* To create these shortcuts, tap Add New Shortcut at the bottom of the Keyboard screen. In the Phrase field, type the words you want to appear, and in the Shortcut field, enter the abbreviation for your phrase. Tap Save, and you'll see your shortcut listed on the Keyboard screen. To use it, open an app that supports text input, such as Notes, and type your shortcut. You'll see it appear as an autofill entry. To expand the shortcut, just tap the spacebar. To ignore it, tap the autofill entry.

International

The International settings screen is where you choose the language for your iPhone or iPod touch, which supports 34 languages. On recent iPhones and iPod touches, you see a Voice Control command below the Language entry. Tap it, and you'll discover that you can speak to your device in any of 24 languages. (There's some overlap in languages, however, because this screen lists English options for three countries: Australia, the United Kingdom, and the United States.) The iPhone or iPod touch not only listens for commands in the language you select, but also tells you what it's doing in a robotic form of that language. VoiceOver, the devices' screen reader, speaks in the language that you choose here.

The Keyboards command appears in the International screen as well. Tap it, and you're taken to your old friend the Keyboards screen, where you can enable additional keyboards.

At the bottom of the International screen, you discover the Region Format and Calendar commands. Tap Region Format, and you can choose among a seemingly endless list of countries supported by the device. Choose a country, and the format for date, time, and telephone number changes. Tap Calendar, and you can choose among four calendar formats: Gregorian, Japanese, Buddhist, and Republic of China.

Accessibility

Apple has taken its world-class VoiceOver technology feature from Mac OS X and adapted it for iOS devices. Now the blind and visually impaired can navigate an iPhone's or iPod touch's touchscreen—something that many people thought would be impossible—thanks to the voice cues and modified commands available on the device.

The ins and outs of accessibility are beyond the scope of this book, but I've written an article, available from Macworld.com, that explains it all. You can find it at http://macw.us/vV9K9A.

Reset

To remove information from your iPhone or iPod touch without syncing it with your computer, you use this screen, which includes a variety of options:

- **Reset All Settings.** This option resets your device's preferences (your Network and Keyboard settings, for example) but doesn't delete media or data (such as your mail settings, bookmarks, and contacts). When you choose this setting, your device restarts.

- **Erase All Content and Settings.** If your iPhone or iPod touch is packed with pirated music, and the Recording Industry Association of America is banging on the door, this option is the one to choose. It erases your preferences and also removes data and media. After you've performed this action, the device will restart as though it's a completely new device. To use it, you'll need to run through the setup procedure again, just as you did when you first unboxed the device.

- **Reset Network Settings.** Choose this option, and any networks you've used are erased, along with your VPN settings. Additionally, the device switches Wi-Fi off and on, thus disconnecting you from the network you're connected to. Yes, this setting is another that restarts your device.

- **Reset Keyboard Dictionary.** As you type on your iPhone's or iPod touch's keyboard, word suggestions occasionally crop up. This feature is really handy when the device guesses the word you're trying to type. If the word is correct, just tap the spacebar, and the word appears complete onscreen. But if the device always guesses particular words incorrectly—your last name, for example—you can correct it by tapping the suggestion and continuing to type. The dictionary will learn that word.

When you tap Reset Keyboard Dictionary, the dictionary returns to its original state, and your additions are erased. Your device doesn't restart, however.

- **Reset Home Screen Layout.** You can move icons on the Home screen around by tapping and holding them until they wiggle, at which point you can move them to another position on that screen or move them to a new screen by dragging them to the right or left edge of the iPhone's or iPod's display. When you invoke this command, the icons on the Home screen return to their default locations, and third-party apps are arranged in alphabetical order.

- **Reset Location Warnings.** An iOS device warns you when an app wants to use the device's Location Services feature. After you OK the warning a second time for a particular app, the iPhone or iPod touch no longer issues the warning for that app. To reset the device so that it starts asking again, invoke this command.

And more

The iPhone and iPod touch includes many more Settings screens—even if you don't count the settings that appear when you install additional apps. Because these settings are tied to specific iPhone or iPod touch functions, I discuss them in the chapters devoted to those subjects.

3

Phone, Messaging, and FaceTime

By now, you likely understand the many hats that the iPhone and iPod touch wear: Internet communicator, music and video player, camera, camcorder, compass, picture viewer, personal information organizer, and pocket computer. But they're also quite adept as communication devices. Although the iPhone has the obvious advantage of being able to make and receive phone calls, the iPod touch is no slouch with regard to two-way communication.

In this chapter, I look at how the two devices help you talk to the world.

Calling All Callers (iPhone Only)

You've synced your contacts to your iPhone, and you're ready to make a call. The iPhone offers multiple ways to do it.

Call the old-fashioned way

Tap the Phone icon on the Home screen to launch the Phone app; then tap the Keypad button at the bottom of the screen to bring up the keypad, if it doesn't open automatically.

On the keypad, tap out the number you want to call. When you enter a number that belongs to someone in your list of contacts, that person's name appears below the number (**Figure 3.1**). Tap Call, and start talking.

Figure 3.1
The old-school keypad.

 tip To bring up the last number you called, tap Keypad. Next, with the number field empty, tap the Call button. Finally, tap Call again.

Connect with Contacts

Tap the Contacts button at the bottom of the Phone screen; locate a contact; tap the contact's name; and in the resulting Info screen, tap the number you want to call. (You can also reach the Contacts screen via the Contacts app within the Utilities folder on your iPhone's Home screen.)

Revisit Recents

If you recently had a phone conversation with someone, that person's number is likely in the Recents list. To find out, tap the Recents button at the bottom of the Phone screen, and seek out the number in the resulting list. When you find that number and/or the contact associated with it, tap the number to place a call.

If the recent call was a FaceTime call (see "Getting a Little FaceTime" later in this chapter), you'll see the word *FaceTime* and a movie-camera icon next to its entry in the Recents list. In that case, tap that entry to initiate a new FaceTime call.

Favor Favorites

If, while browsing through your phone, you added a person to the iPhone's Favorites list (the procedure for which I describe later in the chapter), tap Favorites and then tap that person's name. The iPhone will call her.

Command it (iPhone 3GS and later only)

The iPhone 3GS, iPhone 4, and iPhone 4S can place calls by voice command—and the iPhone 4S can also do many other things via voice, thanks to the new Siri feature, which I discuss in Chapter 1.

With an iPhone 4S, you can simply bring the phone to your ear to engage Siri. Otherwise, as with the iPhone 3GS and iPhone 4, click and hold the Home button until the Voice Control screen appears, and speak these words: "Call Joseph Blow" (*Joseph Blow* being the name of a person in your iPhone's list of contacts). If you have more than one number listed in the intended contact's Info window, you'll be asked which number you'd like to call—Mobile, Home, or Work, for example. Say "Mobile" if you want to call that number, and the call is placed. To avoid this questioning, you can cut to the chase by saying "Call Joseph Blow at home" or "Call Joseph Blow mobile" (**Figure 3.2**).

Figure 3.2
Calling with Voice Control.

tip You'll also avoid further questioning by using the person's full name. Although you can say "Call Jane," if the iPhone has more than one Jane in its list of contacts, you'll be asked which of those many Janes you want to speak with. On the other hand, if you have a friend named Agamemnon or Beelzebub, there's a pretty good chance that you can speak the first name only.

You can also speak a number ("Call 810-555-1212"). Be sure to say the name of each digit—"eight, one, zero" rather than "eight-ten." The iPhone doesn't recognize such shortcuts except in the case of 800, for which you can say "eight hundred" rather than "eight, zero, zero."

If you try any of these techniques when you're out of reach of your phone's cellular network, you'll hear this message: "Voice dialing is unavailable when there is no cellular connection."

Exploring In-Call Options (iPhone Only)

When you place the iPhone against your face while making a call, its screen fades elegantly to black, but its advanced phone features remain at the ready. Pull the phone away from your face, and you'll see a series of option buttons in the middle of the iPhone's screen (**Figure 3.3**). The following sections explain these options.

Figure 3.3
The iPhone's in-call options.

Mute

If your spouse interrupts a call to ask whom you're talking with, I advise you to tap this button before issuing any reply along the lines of "That blowhard Charlie." Doing so turns the Mute button blue and allows you to hear what the other party is saying but mutes the iPhone's microphone. To unmute the phone, just tap Mute again.

Keypad

When a call is in progress, tap this button to display a keypad if you want to enter additional digits. This feature comes in handy for automated phone attendants that require you to enter account numbers, menu choices, and/or your second cousin's height and weight before you can Speak To A Representative. To make the keypad disappear, tap Hide Keypad.

Speaker

The iPhone has speakerphone capabilities. To hear the call from the speaker, tap this button; tap it again to listen to the iPhone's headset or receiver port.

note If your iPhone is paired with a Bluetooth device (a headset or hands-free automobile system, for example), this button is called Audio Source. In this case, tapping the button lets you choose among the Bluetooth device, the iPhone (in wired-headset or against-the-face mode), and the speakerphone.

Add Call

If you've ever tried to create a conference call on another phone, you know how complicated it can be. Not on the iPhone. The process works like this:

1. Tap the Add Call button.

   The person you're speaking with is put on hold. (You might warn her first that you're going to do this.)

2. Place another call.

You can use the keypad (tap the Keypad button to access it) or choose a contact (tap the Contacts button to view your contacts). When that other caller connects, the Add Call button turns into Merge Calls.

3. Tap Merge Calls (**Figure 3.4**).

All three of you will be on the same call.

Figure 3.4
Tap the Merge Calls button to create an instant conference call.

You can add more callers (a conference can have as many as five total callers, including you) by repeating this procedure.

To boot someone from the call, tap the Conference button that appears; tap the red Hang Up button next to the call; and then tap the End Call button that appears.

If you'd like to commiserate privately with one of the other callers in the conference, tap Conference and then tap the Private button next to that caller's name (**Figure 3.5**). When you're ready to rejoin the main call, tap Merge Calls.

Figure 3.5
While you're on a conference call, you can speak privately to one person.

If you'd like to add someone who's calling in to your conference, tap Hold Call + Answer and then tap the Merge Calls button.

Hold

On an iPhone 3G or 3GS, tap the Hold button. On an iPhone 4 or 4S (which lacks a Hold button), tap and hold the Mute button.

FaceTime

If you know that the person you're speaking with is using an iOS device equipped with a camera (or a similarly camera-equipped computer that's also running FaceTime), and he's connected to a Wi-Fi network (because he told you so), you can switch to a FaceTime call by tapping this button. For more info, see "Getting a Little FaceTime" later in this chapter.

Multitask While You're on the Phone

In addition to browsing your contacts while you're on a call, if you're connected to a Wi-Fi or 3G GSM network (but not EDGE), you can do pretty much anything other than use the iPhone's audio functions (including Music and YouTube, as well as any third-party audiocentric applications you may have downloaded from the App Store). Check your stocks, look at the weather in Tasmania, tap out your grocery list, browse your photo collection, or use the Calculator to decide how much you're going to charge this client for taking your time.

When you're ready to hang up or perform some other call-specific action, you can return to the call by tapping the green bar at the top of the iPhone's screen.

Note, however, that CDMA networks such as Verizon's don't allow you to use the iPhone's phone and data features at the same time.

Contacts

As I point out in the "Add Call" section, this button is helpful when you're using the Add Call feature. You can also browse your contacts while you're on a call.

Other buttons and commands

Other buttons can appear during a call, including these:

- **Ignore.** If a call comes in while you're on another call, and you'd rather send it to voice mail than speak with the person, tap the Ignore button.

- **Decline.** To send an incoming call directly to voice mail, press the Sleep/Wake button two times quickly; press the headset's center button for 2 seconds; or tap Decline on the phone.

- **Hold Call + Answer.** To answer that incoming call and put the current caller on hold, tap Hold Call + Answer.

- **End Call + Answer.** For those "Whoops, that's the cheesemonger on the other line. Gotta go!" moments, tap End Call + Answer to drop the current call and answer the incoming call.

- **Swap.** You've put the Party of the First Part on hold to speak with the Party of the Second Part. To return to the PotFP and hold the PotSP, tap Swap, or tap the first caller's entry at the top of the screen.

- Emergency Call. I hope you never have to tap this button. The iPhone, like all mobile phones in the United States, can make emergency calls to special numbers (911, for example) when you're out of range of the network and even if your phone doesn't have a SIM card installed. But if you've locked your phone with a passcode and don't have time to unlock it, bring up the keypad, tap the Emergency Call button, and then tap out the emergency number.

Phone Settings

The iPhone lets you take advantage of special calling features built into your plan. The means for managing those features is the Phone screen, which you access via the Settings screen. Tap Phone in this screen, and you'll see these options:

- **My Number.** By default, your iPhone's phone number appears next to the My Number entry. Interestingly enough, you can change it to a different number. Just tap the number, and up pops the My Number screen. You're welcome to tap the X icon to erase what's in the field and enter a different number—your landline number, for example.

- **FaceTime.** This On/Off toggle option allows you to disable the iPhone's video-calling feature. (See "Get a little FaceTime" earlier in this chapter for more details.)

- **Call Forwarding.** Tap it to access the On/Off slider.

- **Call Waiting.** Ditto.

- **Show My Caller ID.** If you don't want people to know who's calling (or the number you're calling from), flip this option on.

- **TTY.** This accessibility feature allows you to connect your iPhone to a compatible TTY (teletype) machine via the optional iPhone TTY Adapter cable. People use this technology to create messages that can be read by the deaf and hearing-impaired.

- **Change Voicemail Password.** Tap this option, and you'll be prompted for your current voice-mail password (actually, a passcode; on the iPhone, voice-mail passwords are numeric). Enter it successfully and tap the Done button, and you proceed to the next screen, where you enter a new password. Tap Done again, and you're asked to confirm your new password by entering it one more time.

(Continues on next page)

Phone Settings (continued)

- **International Assist.** Enable this option, and when you take your iPhone overseas, you can call numbers in your home country without having to preface them with prefix or country codes.

- **SIM PIN.** It's possible to lock your iPhone's Subscriber Information Module (SIM)—the small card inserted into your iPhone that carries some of the phone's personal and subscriber information—with a personal identification number (PIN). Lock the SIM card, and no one can use the phone to make a call without entering the correct PIN.

- **AT&T Services (U.S. only).** Tap AT&T Services in the Phone settings screen, and you get a list of shortcut numbers that you can call for various services, including Check Bill Balance, Directory Assistance, Pay My Bill, View My Minutes, and Voice Connect. Tap any of these shortcuts, and the iPhone sends a request for that information to AT&T. Then AT&T responds with a text message containing the information you requested.

Managing Your Calling Plan (iPhone Only)

When the iPhone first hit the street, Apple placed the Phone application's icon in prime position: in the first spot among the four major apps at the bottom of the Home screen. Tap that Phone icon, and you see one of the five Phone application screens: Favorites, Recents, Contacts, Keypad, or Voicemail. (Which screen appears depends on the last one you accessed before moving back to the Home screen or to another application.) A row of buttons at the bottom of all five screens (refer to Figure 3.1) lets you navigate quickly among these screens. Because you may be in a hurry to place a call, I'll discuss them out of order.

Keypad

The function of this button couldn't be much more obvious. Tap Keypad, and you see ... a telephone keypad. To place a call, just tap the digits you want. As you tap, each digit appears in order at the top of the screen, nicely formatted with the area code in parentheses followed by the number—*(555) 555-1212*, for example.

In addition to the number keys, star (*), and pound (#), the keypad includes these buttons:

- **Add Contact.** The Add Contact button lets you create a contact quickly, based on the number you've tapped in.

  Suppose that your dentist calls and leaves a message: He needs a new boat, and your previously unmentioned impacted wisdom tooth will help him with the down payment. He asks you to call him back at 555-1234. You tap in the number, tap Add Contact, and then choose Create New Contact if you have no contact for him or Add to Existing Contact if you don't have his new office number. (Or you can tap Cancel if you've thought better of the whole thing.)

- **Call.** Tap Call to call the number you've entered.

- **Delete.** Tap Delete to erase the last digit you entered. Tap and hold to delete a string of numbers quickly.

Voicemail

The iPhone offers a unique voice-mail system dubbed Visual Voicemail. What makes it different from other phones' systems is that you needn't wade through half a dozen messages to get to the one you really want to hear. Instead, all received messages appear in a list, and you tap just the ones you want to listen to.

No one can be available 24 hours a day, so here's how to set up and use voice mail when you're not available to take a call:

1. Tap the Voicemail button at the bottom of the Phone screen.

When you first tap Voicemail, you'll be prompted to enter a password and record a voice greeting. (When recording that greeting, it's not a bad idea to be somewhere quiet with good phone reception so that your greeting is as clear as possible.)

If you don't care to record a greeting, tap Voicemail > Greeting and then tap the Default button. Callers will hear a canned greeting put together by your carrier.

note To create a greeting at another time, just tap the Greeting button at the top of the Voicemail screen and then tap Custom. Tap Record; say your piece; then tap Done. Tap Play to listen to what you've recorded, and if you like it, tap Save.

2. Locate a message you want to hear.

Messages are named for the person who called (if known). The time (or date, if the call was made on a different day) appears next to the caller's name. A blue arrow icon appears next to each name, even if that name is *Unknown;* tap that icon to be taken to a contact Info screen. A blue dot marks each unheard message.

3. Select the message you want to listen to, and tap the Play button on the left side of the message entry.

The Play button changes to Pause while the iPhone downloads the message and then plays it (**Figure 3.6**).

Figure 3.6
Playing a voice-mail message.

To pause a playing message, tap the Pause button (the two vertical lines) to the left of the caller's name. Tap the Play symbol (the right-pointing triangle) to resume playing the message.

When you begin playing a message, a new sheet appears, displaying a scrubber bar and Call Back and Delete buttons. To move through a message quickly—if your father tends to go on and on about this season's gopher issues before getting to the meat of the message, for example—drag the playhead to a later point in the message. If the phone was able to obtain a number through Caller ID, you have the option to call that person back immediately by tapping Call Back.

To listen to a message again, simply select it again and tap the Play button. If listening once was enough, tap Delete.

note Deleted messages aren't completely gone. At the end of your voice-mail list, you'll see a Deleted Messages entry. Tap this entry and then tap the message you'd like to listen to again. You can undelete a message by tapping it in the Deleted Messages screen and then tapping Undelete.

4. (Optional) Create a contact.

If someone who isn't in your list of contacts calls, and you'd like to add her to that list, tap the blue arrow icon next to the message heading. In the sheet that appears, tap either Create New Contact (if this contact is new to you) or Add to Existing Contact (if the caller is already a contact, but you don't have this particular number). Then choose a contact to add the number to.

If you've created a contact for a caller, you can also add her to your Favorites list, which I describe in greater detail later in this chapter. Just tap the blue arrow icon and then tap Add to Favorites.

5. (Also optional) Listen later.

The iPhone lets you know if you have voice-mail messages waiting. If you've missed one or more calls, received one or more voice-mail messages, or both, a red circle appears in the top-right corner of the Phone application's icon on the Home screen. A number inside the circle denotes the combined number of missed calls and unheard messages. When you tap the Phone icon, a similar red circle appears over the Voicemail icon, indicating how many unheard messages you have.

Recents

Like other modern mobile phones, the iPhone keeps track of calls you've made and received—both those you've participated in and those you've missed. You'll find a list of those most recent calls by tapping the Recents button at the bottom of the Phone screen.

In the Recents screen, you may see any (or all) of the following:

- **Names,** if the callers or recipients are in your phone's list of contacts

  If a name appears, you'll also see the kind of number the call came from (mobile, home, work, or FaceTime, for example).

- **Phone numbers,** if the callers or recipients aren't in the phone's list of contacts and the numbers aren't blocked

    For a number, you also see the location of the number (such as Anytown, AK).

- **The word** *blocked,* if a phone number is blocked

Contacts that you've attempted to reach multiple times have a number next to them—*Jane Blow (3)* or *555-1243 (2)*, for example—indicating the number of calls made.

To see all calls, tap the All button at the top of the screen (**Figure 3.7**). Missed calls are shown in red. To see just your missed calls, tap the Missed button at the top of the screen. As in Voicemail, you see the time or day when the call was made. Tap the blue arrow icon to be taken to one of a few screens, depending on what your iPhone "knows" about the phone number for each call you've placed or received.

Figure 3.7
The Recents screen.

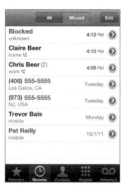

If a number belongs to someone listed in your contacts, tapping the blue arrow icon takes you to a screen that displays that person's contact info. Additionally, you see the kind of call (outgoing or incoming), the time and date of the call, and the length of the call. (This entry reads *Cancelled* if the call didn't go through.) At the bottom of that screen are icons marked Send Message, Share Contact, FaceTime, and Add to Favorites. You use them as follows:

- **Send Message.** Tap Send Message to launch the Messages app and open a blank text message directed to that person. (If the person has more than one phone number or email account in her contact info, a sheet appears and asks you to choose the number to use.)

- **Share Contact.** When you tap Share Contact, a sheet rolls up to offer you three options: Email, Message, and Cancel. When you tap Email, a new, unaddressed email message opens, containing that person's contact information saved as a vCard attachment. (vCard is a universal format for exchanging contact information between devices.) To send that message, just enter a recipient in the To field and type something in the Subject field. (You can learn far more about email and the iPhone in Chapter 4.) Tap Message, and a new message opens in the Messages application, containing the vCard as part of that message, or tap Cancel to do the obvious.

- **FaceTime.** Tap FaceTime, and your iPhone attempts to make a FaceTime video call. (For details, see "Getting a Little FaceTime" later in this chapter.)

- **Add to Favorites.** Tap Add to Favorites, and that's just what happens: The person is added to your list of favorites, and you can access his info by tapping Favorites at the bottom of the screen.

If you place a call to a number that isn't in the iPhone's list of contacts, or if you capture an unrecognized Caller ID number from a received call, the phone number is displayed, and you can tap the blue arrow icon to view these options: Call, Message, Create New Contact, Add to Existing Contact, and Share Contact.

If the number came from a blocked number, the entry reads *Blocked Caller*, and tapping the icon tells you only the date and time when the person called.

Tap Clear to clear the Recents lists.

Favorites

Use the Favorites list to store those very special contacts you call routinely (**Figure 3.8**). Here, you'll find the numbers you've added by tapping the Add to Favorites button in a contact's Info screen or by tapping Favorites, tapping the plus (+) icon, and then navigating through your list of contacts to find a name. You can add only contacts that have an associated phone number (for calling) or email address (for FaceTime).

Figure 3.8
The Favorites screen.

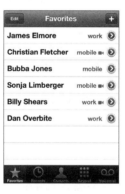

Just like those in Recents and Voicemail, each entry in the Favorites list bears a small blue arrow icon. Tap it to view that person's Info screen.

Contacts

Last but hardly least is Contacts. Because your friends, relatives, and associates are the worthiest people on Earth, they deserve their own section, which comes up right away.

Working with Contacts

Although contacts are clearly important on the iPhone, when you need to locate someone's name and phone number quickly, they're useful on an iPod touch as well, as you'll want to pull up contacts for map locations as well as find people's FaceTime addresses. You'll find it more convenient to ask your address-book application to do the heavy lifting with regard to creating and editing contacts (because it's far easier to enter information on a real keyboard than on the iPhone's or iPod touch's virtual keyboard), but you can do a lot of worthwhile things with contacts directly on one of these devices.

Entering the people you know

Launch the Contacts app (or, on an iPhone, tap the Contacts icon at the bottom of the Phone app's screen), and you see your contacts listed in alphabetical order (**Figure 3.9**), with a Search field at the top of the screen for seeking out contacts.

Figure 3.9
The Contacts screen.

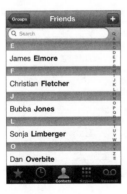

The Contacts list works very much like any long list of items you'd see in the Music app. A tiny alphabet runs down the right side of the screen. Tap a letter to move immediately to contacts whose names (first or last, depending on how you've configured name sorting in the Contacts preferences screen) begin with this letter. Alternatively, tap the Search field, and when the keyboard swoops up from the bottom of the screen, start typing some letters in your contact's name. As you type, fewer names appear as the choices narrow.

When you tap a name, you're taken to that contact's Info screen (**Figure 3.10**). Here, you can find information including the following:

Figure 3.10
A contact's Info screen.

- Photo

  This item can be a photo you've added by importing it from Address Book on a Mac, by tapping Add Photo and choosing a picture from your Photos application, or by assigning a picture to a contact in the Photos or Camera app.

- Name

- Company

- Phone number

  Possible phone headings include (but aren't limited to) Mobile, iPhone, Home, Work, Main, Home Fax, Work Fax, Pager, and Other.

- Email address

  This item includes Home, Work, and Other options, as well as any custom labels you've created.

- Ringtone

- Vibration (iPhone only)

- Text tone (iPhone only)

- URL (for the contact's Web site)

- Address

- Other fields

You won't necessarily find all these entries in a contact's Info screen; this list just shows you what's possible to include.

Organizing contacts in groups

Although you see a list of all your contacts when you first tap Contacts, the Contacts application has an organizational layer above the main list. If, in the Info preference within iTunes, you've chosen to sync your address book with select groups of contacts, or if your full address book contains groups of contacts, those groups appear in the Groups screen, which you access by tapping the Groups button in the top-left corner of the Contacts screen (**Figure 3.11**).

Figure 3.11
The Groups screen.

Organizing in groups makes a lot of sense if you have loads of contacts. Although Apple made traversing a long list of contacts as easy as possible, easier still is tapping something like a Family group and picking Uncle Bud's name out of a list of 17 beloved relatives.

Making contacts

The best way to become familiar with iPhone and iPod touch contacts is to make some of your own. To do that now, launch the Contacts app and then tap the plus (+) icon in the top-right corner of the screen.

Viewing the New Contact screen

The New Contact screen contains fields for the elements I list in "Entering the people you know" earlier in this chapter, as well as an Add Field entry (**Figure 3.12**). To add information to one of these fields, tap the field or the green plus icon to its left. In the resulting screen, you'll find a place to enter the information.

Figure 3.12
The New Contact screen.

Here are the special features of each screen:

Add Photo. Tap this entry to display a sheet containing buttons marked Take Photo, Choose Photo, and Cancel. Tap Take Photo, point it at the object you'd like to capture, and tap the green camera icon. If you need help with using the Camera app's interfaces, see Chapter 8.

Why all the fuss about a contact's picture when it appears in this tiny box? If you've attached a photo to a contact, that photo occupies much of the iPhone's or iPod touch's screen when that person calls you on the phone or via FaceTime.

First and Last Name. In these fields, you enter first and last names.

Company. Enter a company name in this field, if you like.

Phone. As the name implies, this field is where you add a phone number. By default, the sole entry is Mobile. To choose a different kind of phone, tap Mobile; a Label sheet scrolls up from the bottom of the display, letting you choose options from a long list. If you've added any custom labels on the device, in Apple's Address Book (Mac), or in Outlook (Windows), those custom labels appear below the preceding entries. At the very bottom of the sheet, you'll find an Add Custom Label button that, when tapped, lets you type a label of your own making—*Dirigible* or *Private Train Car*, for example.

note The numeric keypad contains a key that reads +*#. Tap it, and these three characters appear on the keypad's bottom three keys, along with the word *pause*, which enters a comma (,) character. What good are they? They're used by automated answering systems for performing certain functions. Some phone systems, for example, require you to press the pound key and then a key combination to unblock a hidden phone number or append an extension. The comma character is commonly used to insert a 1-second delay. It's useful when an automated answering service demands that you wait a second before punching in another string of numbers.

Email. Enter your contact's email addresses here. The device's keyboard in this screen contains @ and period (.) keys to make the process easier. Tap and hold the period key, and a menu appears that contains .net, .edu, .org, .us, and .com. Just slide your finger over to the extension you want, and let go to enter it. As with adding a phone number, you can tap the Home entry and choose a different name from the Label sheet that appears.

Ringtone. You can choose a unique ringtone for each contact, and here's where you do it. Tap Ringtone, and the default ringtone for your device appears at the top of the ringtone list with a check mark next to it. You can choose a different ringtone from the list below—a list that includes the 25 ringtones and 27 alert sounds bundled with your device, followed by any custom ringtones you've added via iTunes' Ringtones tab. If you have an iPhone, this feature is a great way to know who's calling without having to pull the phone out of your pocket.

Vibration (iPhone only). In Chapter 2, I describe how to create a custom vibration on your iPhone. This entry is the doorway to that feature. Tap Vibration and then choose one of the five bundled vibration patterns, create or choose one of your own, or choose None.

Text Tone. As with other audio alerts, choose a different ringtone, alert, or custom sound here.

Home Page. This entry is for entering the URL (Web address) associated with the contact. Here, too, the keyboard has been changed to be more convenient for entering Web addresses, in that it contains period (.), slash (/), and .com keys. You can apply a Home Page, Home, Work, or Other label to the URL, as well as any custom labels on your phone.

Add New Address. In the United States, the default Edit Address screen contains Street, City, State, and Zip fields. Ah, but if you tap the Country field and choose a different nation from the list that appears, the other fields change. If you choose Belarus, for example, the fields include Street, Postal Code, City, and Province. Tap the Location icon next to the Country icon to choose the nature of this address: Home, Work, or Other and (as you might expect) one of those custom labels.

Add Field. Tap Add Field, and you can add more fields to a contact's Info screen. These fields include Prefix, Phonetic First Name, Phonetic Last Name, Middle, Suffix, Nickname, Job Title, Department, Twitter, Profile, Instant Message, Birthday, Date (Anniversary and Other are the options), Related People, and Notes. Both the Birthday and Date screens contain the device's spinning date wheel for selecting the month, day, and year quickly.

Managing existing contacts

When you have contacts on your iPhone or iPod touch, you can delete them, edit the information they contain, or use that information to perform other tasks on your device.

To delete a contact, just tap the Edit button that appears in the contact's Info screen, scroll to the bottom of the screen, and tap the big red Delete Contact button. You'll be asked to confirm your choice.

To edit a contact, tap that same Edit button in the contact's Info screen, and make the edits you want (**Figure 3.13**). You can add information by tapping a field that begins with the word *Add* (or just tap its green plus icon). To delete information, tap the red minus (–) icon next to the information and then tap the now-revealed Delete button. When you're finished editing the contact, tap Done.

Figure 3.13
A contact edit screen.

As for initiating actions on your iPhone or iPod touch via a contact's Info screen, most of the elements in the screen are *live*, meaning that if you tap them, something happens. If you tap a phone number in the Info screen on an iPhone, for example, the iPhone dials that number;

tap an email address, and a New Message window appears in the Mail application, addressed to that person. If you tap a URL, Safari opens and takes you to that Web page. Tap an address, and Maps opens to show you its location.

At the bottom of an Info screen that contains at least one phone number, you'll find Send Message, Share Contact, FaceTime, and Add to Favorites buttons. Because Message, FaceTime, and Add to Favorites require a phone number or email address, you can see why they're present here but not in Info screens that don't bear phone numbers or email addresses. Share Contact appears for all contacts and, again, offers you the option to send an email or message that contains that person's contact information in the form of a vCard.

You already know about favorites. When you tap Send Message, if the contact has more than one phone number or email address in the Info screen, a sheet rolls up that contains each phone number and email address. Tap the number or address you'd like to use, and the Messages application opens, with the contact's name at the top of the screen.

And gosh, speaking of messages...

Sending Them Messages

When Steve Jobs first demoed the iPhone, it appeared to contain an instant-messaging client similar to Apple's iChat. That turned out not to be the case. The iPhone's SMS (Short Message Service) application, Messages (formerly called Text), looks very much like iChat, but it's not. It's a standard messaging service, much like the ones you find on other mobile phones. Some years later, the iPhone added support for MMS (Multimedia Messaging Service)—a way to send not just text messages, but also messages that can include audio, video, pictures, and rich text.

You can't blame iPod touch owners for being a little bent out of shape that they didn't also enjoy this kind of messaging service. But text messages are only for mobile phones, right? As it turns out, no. With iOS 5, Apple introduced a new version of Messages that works not only with the iPhone, but also with the iPod touch.

It can do this because, like FaceTime, Messages doesn't require a phone number to work. On an iPod touch, you can send messages to another iOS device as long as you have the email address associated with that other device and you're connected to a Wi-Fi network. These non-SMS messages are called *iMessages* (but the app is still called Messages— confusing, I know). Likewise, others can send iMessages to you if they have the correct email address. With an iPhone, you can use either an email address or the traditional method of sending messages to a phone number.

The best thing about this feature is that it's completely free. Even if you send an iMessage from an iPhone, if you do so by sending it to an email address rather than a phone number, that message doesn't count against the text-message limit imposed by your cellular carrier.

Configuring the Messages app

To use Messages, you must have an Apple ID. If you entered that ID when you first configured your iPhone or iPod touch, Messages will use the email address associated with it. If you didn't enter an Apple ID, just tap the Messages app's icon to launch it; you'll be prompted to enter your Apple ID or create a new one by tapping the Create New Account button. In the succeeding screen, you'll be offered the choice to use the address associated with your Apple ID. If you prefer to use a different address, tap the Address field and enter it with the device's keyboard. When you're done, tap Next. Your address will be verified, and when it is, you'll see a New Message screen.

If you'd like to change this address later, simply launch the Settings app, tap Messages, and then tap the address that appears in the Receive At field in the resulting screen. In the next screen, titled iMessage, tap the Email field and enter a new email address. Alternatively, add another email address by tapping Add Another Email Address and then entering the address in the Email field that appears.

tip   Why have more than one email address associated with Messages? You may not care to share your personal email address with your colleagues at work or your work email address with certain friends. If you have multiple Messages addresses, you can still message people without spilling the beans about email accounts that you'd like to keep private.

Sending text messages

Using Messages is pretty straightforward. Just follow these steps:

1. Tap Messages on the device's Home screen.

    You see the Messages screen.

2. Tap the New Message button in the top-right corner of the screen.

    In the resulting New Messages screen, the cursor is placed in a To field, ready for you to address the message.

3. To enter a name in this field, begin typing the name of the person you want to message—or, if you have an iPhone 4S, tap the keyboard's Microphone key and say the name.

    As you type, a list of matching names from your contacts list appears (**Figure 3.14**). Continue to type, and the list narrows.

Figure 3.14
Start typing a name, and your iPhone or iPod touch suggests recipients.

4. To select a recipient, just tap that person's name.

   Alternatively, you can tap the plus icon in the To field, which brings up the contacts list. Navigate to the contact you want to contact, and tap that person's name to add it to the To field.

   Finally, if you have an iPod touch, you can enter an email address that you know is associated with an iMessage account; if you have an iPhone, you can enter a phone number or email address that's capable of receiving a message.

5. To add another recipient, simply tap the To field and start typing, just as you did before.

   Regrettably, there's no way to send a message to an existing group in Contacts; you must add addresses one by one.

6. Tap the text field, and start typing—or, again, if you have an iPhone 4S, tap the Microphone button and dictate your message.

   The field can display seven lines of text before the first line scrolls out of sight.

7. When you're ready to send your message, tap Send (**Figure 3.15**).

Figure 3.15
A message session in progress.

**tip** By default, to save you money, an iPhone attempts to send a message to an email address rather than using SMS. Within the Messages setting screen is a Send As SMS switch, which is initially set to On. If you don't want Messages to send an SMS message after it fails to send a message to a contact's email address, turn this switch off.

---

iMessages vs. SMS Messages

It's easy to tell the difference between iMessages and SMS messages. iMessages (the free ones) you send are presented in a blue bubble, and the text field reads **iMessage**. Messages in a green bubble (as in the color of money in the United States) that you send are SMS messages that you pay for. When you're communicating via SMS, the text field reads **Text Message**. Messages that you receive are always in a gray bubble.

Sending MMS messages

Sending an MMS message isn't much different from sending a text message. Launch Messages, and tap the New Message button in the top-right corner of the Message screen. You'll see a small camera icon next to the Send field. This button is for sending still images or movies via MMS.

Sending images or video

Sending an image or video is simple. On an iOS device that has a camera, a sheet appears, offering three buttons: Take Photo or Video, Choose Existing, and Cancel. (If you have an older iOS device without a camera, you see a Photos window instead and can choose an image there.)

Tap Take a Photo or Video, and the Camera app launches. (In Chapter 8, I explain how to use the Camera app.) If you're already familiar with it, you're well on your way. Just tap the Camera/Record button to capture what you want, and if you like what you've taken, tap Use (or Retake if you'd like to try again). The image or movie is attached to your message, ready to send.

If you tap the second button—Choose Existing—the Photo Albums screen appears, listing all the photos and videos on your iPhone or iPod touch.

> **tip** I find it helpful to add a subject heading to messages that contain images or movies. You can expose a Subject field by tapping Messages in the Settings screen and flicking the Show Subject Field switch to On. Then, to enter a subject, return to the Messages app; tap the Subject field that appears above your attached media; and enter a subject.

Sending audio

As I mention earlier in this chapter, you can also send audio files that you've recorded with the Voice Memos application via MMS. I cover voice memos more extensively in Chapter 9, but while I'm on the subject of MMS, here's the gist:

1. Launch Voice Memos.

   By default in iOS 4 and iOS 5, you'll find this app's icon in the Utilities folder on the device's Home screen.

2. Tap the red Record button, and start speaking to record your memo.

3. Tap the button in the bottom-right corner of the screen (which displays a black square during recording) to stop recording.

4. Tap that same button, which now displays three lines, to open the Voice Memos screen.

5. Tap a voice memo that you'd like to use as an MMS message.

6. Tap the Share button at the bottom of the screen and then tap the Message button that appears.

   Messages launches, with your voice memo embedded in the Send field of a new message (**Figure 3.16**).

Figure 3.16
A voice memo embedded in an MMS message.

7. Address the message.

8. Enter a subject (if you've switched on that option in the Messages setting screen; see the tip in the preceding section).

9. Tap Send to send the audio MMS message.

Receiving messages

When it receive a message, the iPhone or iPod touch alerts you through a notification. The kind of notification you get depends on how you've configured the Notification setting. An iPod touch can alert you in multiple ways at the same time: You can hear a sound, see an alert or banner, view the notification in the Lock screen, and see a badge on the Messages icon that indicates the number of unread messages. The iPhone can additionally notify you by vibrating when it receives a message.

To view your messages, just tap the Messages app or the alert you just received. If you tap the Messages app, you should see a list of all the messages you've received, with unread messages marked with blue dots. If you tap an alert, you'll be taken directly to the message that just came in.

Sending replies

Regardless of how you navigate to a message, to reply to it, you enter the text in the Send field with the device's keyboard and then tap Send. (The MMS Camera icon appears next to this field as well.) If you'd like to let other people know that you've read their messages, open the Messages setting, and enable the Send Read Receipts option.

Make the keyboard disappear by swiping down in the message area, and you'll see some buttons at the top of the screen. Which buttons you see depend on who the sender is and the kind of device you're using. If you have an iPhone, and you're texting with someone over SMS, those buttons read Call, FaceTime, and Add Contact (if this person isn't in your list of contacts) or Contact (if she's in your contacts). If you're using iMessage to text, the first button reads Email. On an iPod touch, you don't have the option to call the person, so the buttons read Email, FaceTime, and either Add Contact or Contact.

The buttons do exactly what they suggest. Tap Call on an iPhone, and you place a call to this contact. Tap Email, and a new email message appears, addressed to that person. Tap FaceTime to initiate a FaceTime call (if you're connected to a Wi-Fi network). Tap Add Contact to either create a new contact or add information to an existing contact. Finally, tap Contact to view the person's contact information stored on your device.

Deleting and forwarding messages

To delete entries from the Messages list, just tap the Edit button; then tap the red minus icon, and tap Delete. The swipe-and-delete trick works here, too. Just swipe your finger to the left or right across the message entry, and tap the Delete button that appears.

You can also delete or forward portions of a message conversation. To do so, follow these steps:

1. Tap a conversation that you'd like to edit.

   It appears in a separate screen, with the name of the recipient at the top.

2. Tap the Edit button in the top-right corner.

3. Tap the circle next to the portions of the conversation that you want to delete or forward.

4. Delete the selected portion by tapping the Delete button at the bottom of the window.

5. To forward a selection, tap the Forward button.

When you tap Forward, a New Message screen appears.

6. In the To field, add the recipients and/or phone numbers (if you're using an iPhone) for your forwarded message.

7. When you're ready to send the forwarded message, just tap the Send button.

Messages can also contain live links. If someone places a phone number in a message, for example, and if you have an iPhone, you can tap that number to call it. (This shortcut won't work on an iPod touch, of course.) Email addresses, URLs, and physical addresses are live too. Tap an email address, and Mail opens with a message addressed to that person. Tap a URL, and Safari launches, taking you to that site. Tap a street address, and Maps opens to reveal that location in Google Maps. And, of course, media such as still images, videos, and audio files appear and/or play in all their glory when tapped.

Getting a Little FaceTime

Today's iPhones and iPod touches carry a front-facing camera, and the main reason they do is to allow you to participate in video calls with friends, family members, and colleagues. Apple terms this video-calling technology *FaceTime*. To use it, each participant must have a compatible iOS device (iPhone 4, iPhone 4S, or 4G iPod touch, or iPad 2) and a Wi-Fi connection. Only two people can participate in a FaceTime call; conference calling isn't supported.

note FaceTime works only over Wi-Fi, not 3G or EDGE. If you wander out of range of a Wi-Fi network, the video conversation ends, and on an iPhone, you're offered the option to redial the number to make a voice call.

Setting up FaceTime

To set up FaceTime, follow these steps:

1. Launch Settings.

2. Tap the FaceTime entry.

3. In the resulting screen, ensure that the FaceTime switch is set to On.

4. Do one of the following:

   ▪ Tap the button labeled Use Your Apple ID for FaceTime if you'd like that email address to be associated with FaceTime.

     If you have an iPhone, you don't need to associate an email address with FaceTime. People who want to contact you via FaceTime can simply use the device's phone number. But tapping this button makes it easy to add the email address associated with your Apple ID.

     On an iPod touch, you don't have a phone number, so you must enter an email address. This address is the one that other people will use to contact you via FaceTime, so you'll want to be sure to pass it to your friends, relatives, and colleagues.

   ▪ If you don't want to use the address associated with your Apple ID, tap the Add an Email field, and enter the email address you want to use.

     As I mention earlier in the chapter, you can use more than one email address. When you do, a Caller ID entry appears at the bottom of the FaceTime settings screen. Tap it, and you can set the address that will appear on the screen of the person you're calling.

Making a FaceTime call

Now that you have FaceTime configured, you're ready to make a call. Here's how:

1. Select a contact in the Contacts app or (on an iPhone) within the contacts area of the Phone app.

2. Scroll to the bottom of the contact screen, and tap the FaceTime button.

   The FaceTime screen appears, with the contact's name displayed at the top. (If the contact has multiple phone numbers and/or email addresses, a sheet appears first; you choose the entry associated that person has associated with FaceTime.)

3. Wait while the iPhone or iPod touch contacts your contact.

   If the number you're attempting to contact isn't associated with an iOS device, or if the person who has that number has blocked FaceTime calls (see the note at the end of this section), you'll see a message that your call has failed.

   If the contact chooses to answer the call (by tapping the Accept button that appears on his device's screen), his video image appears, taking up most of your iPhone's or iPod touch's screen (**Figure 3.17**). In one corner, you see a small picture-in-picture image of yourself, which lets you position yourself properly in the frame. You can drag that image to any corner of the display.

4. Hold the device so that the person you're speaking with can see you, and talk normally.

   FaceTime can use both portrait and landscape orientation, so you're free to rotate the device as you talk; the iPhone or iPod touch rotates the FaceTime image accordingly.

Figure 3.17
*The FaceTime
screen.*

note FaceTime uses the microphone that's built into the device, so be sure to avoid putting your finger over the mic. Also watch that you don't obscure the camera lens with a misplaced digit.

5. During the call, feel free to use any of FaceTime's in-call options:

   - **Mute the call.** You can mute the call by tapping the Mute button in the bottom-left corner of the screen. The person with whom you're speaking will still see you but won't hear you.

   - **Switch cameras.** If you want to show off what's going on around you, you can switch to the device's rear-facing camera by tapping the Camera Swap button in the bottom-right corner of the screen. To switch back to the front-facing camera, just tap that button again.

   - **Switch apps.** If you need to dash to another application during a FaceTime call—to look up a contact or make a note, for example— you can do that by clicking the Home button and then opening the app you want. This action interrupts the video portion of the call, but audio still works; you can hear and be heard. When you're ready to return to the video call, just tap the green bar at the top of the device's display.

6. To end the call, tap the End button.

That End button appears on both devices, so either party can end the call.

note There will be times when you're not ready to receive a FaceTime call. (Not all of us look our best at 6 a.m. on a Saturday, after all.) You can disable FaceTime easily by launching the Settings app, tapping the FaceTime preference, and switching off the FaceTime option. (You can also turn off FaceTime in the Restrictions section of the General settings screen.)

4

Mail, Calendar, and Reminders

Seeking an electronic means for staying in touch while on the go? Can't figure out how to copy the notes and photos from your iPhone or iPod touch to a computer that's not synced with your device, or how to receive documents that you can view on that device? Or is your life so tied to email that you can't stand to be away from your computer for more than a couple of hours? If so, you and the Mail application are about to become best friends.

Portable email is a real boon, and so is knowing where you're supposed to be from one minute to the next. To help with the latter, the iPhone and iPod touch include a Calendar app that lets you sync your schedule with your Mac or Windows PC, as well as create calendar events on the go. And now, thanks to iOS 5, you can create and keep track of to-do items in the new Reminders app. In this chapter, I explain the ins and outs of all three apps.

Using Mail

Mail is a real email client, much like the one you use on your computer. With it, you can send and receive email messages, as well as send and receive a limited variety of email attachments. With Mail, you can view email from all the accounts set up on your device in a single unified inbox. If you have iCloud, Google, and Yahoo email accounts, for example, you can launch the Mail app; tap the All Inboxes entry; and see all the messages you've received, regardless of which of these three accounts they were sent to.

The Mail app also lets you send photos or videos you've taken with your device's camera, as well as receive and play such audio attachments as MP3, AAC, WAV, and AIFF. You can view received JPEG graphics, text files, and HTML files; Microsoft Word, Excel, and PowerPoint documents; iWork Pages, Keynote, and Numbers files; and Adobe PDF documents. As you can on any iOS device, you can choose to open (and, in some cases, edit) some attachments with a third-party app. You do this by tapping the attachment and then, in the sheet that appears, selecting the app from a list. The attachment opens in that app, ready for viewing and editing.

Mail is limited in some other ways:

- Unlike all other modern computer-based email clients, the iPhone and iPod touch have no spam filter and no feature for managing mailing lists.

- You can't apply rules that allow Mail to sort or copy certain messages (those from a particular sender, for example) to specific mailboxes.

- You can't clear out a mailbox by deleting all its messages in one fell swoop. You have to select individual messages and then delete them.

- With an iPod touch, you can send and receive email only over a Wi-Fi connection. Unlike the iPhone, the iPod touch has no cellular modem, so 3G and EDGE networks (which rely on such modems) aren't available.

Now that you know what Mail can and can't do, you're ready to look at how to use it.

Creating an account

When you first configured your device, you were offered the opportunity to create an iCloud account. If you've done that, you already have an email account set up on your device—one for iCloud. Likewise, if you've already synced your iPhone or iPod touch, you had the chance to synchronize your email account to the device. If you chose to do so, your iPhone or iPod touch is nearly ready to send and receive messages. All you may have to do now is enter a password for your email account in the Mail, Contacts, Calendars screen.

But I'm getting ahead of myself. Rather than start in the middle, with a nearly configured account, I'll start at the beginning so that you can follow the device's account-setup procedure from start to finish. In the next few pages, I examine how to configure iCloud, Microsoft Exchange accounts, Web-based accounts (Gmail, Yahoo, AOL, Hotmail, and MobileMe), and IMAP and POP accounts.

Configuring an Exchange account

Those of you who use corporate Exchange accounts can add them to your devices too, as follows:

1. Tap Settings > Mail, Contacts, Calendars.

2. Tap Add Account (located in the Accounts list).

3. In the resulting screen, tap Microsoft Exchange to open an Exchange screen.

4. Enter your email address, user name, password, and a description (perhaps along the lines of *Company Email*).

Your IT department or manager should be able to provide this info.

5. Tap Next.

The iPhone or iPod touch attempts to connect to the Exchange server.

If the connection is successful, you're pretty well set. If it isn't, another Exchange screen asks for the same information you provided in step 4, as well as the server address. Again, the Exchange server administrator should be able to give you this information. The address in question here is the address of the front-end server—the one that greets your device when it attempts to connect to the company server.

When this information is configured properly, the iPhone or iPod touch attempts to log on to the server via a Secure Sockets Layer (SSL) connection. If it can't do so, it tries a nonsecure connection.

note If SSL isn't configured correctly, you can change those settings by tapping the name of your Exchange account in the Mail, Contacts, Calendars screen; tapping Account Info; and flipping the SSL slider to On or Off, depending on how it should be configured.

6. When you're prompted to choose the kinds of data—Mail, Contacts, or Calendars—that you want to synchronize between your device and the Exchange server, flick the switches for those data types to On (**Figure 4.1**).

Figure 4.1
*Choose the kinds
of data you want
to sync with the
Exchange server.*

By default, the iPhone and iPod touch synchronize just three days'
worth of email. If you need to store more email on your device, select
your Exchange account in the Mail, Contacts, Calendars screen; tap
Mail Days to Sync; and choose a new number of days' worth of email
to synchronize. Your options are No Limit, 1 Day, 3 Days, 1 Week, 2 Weeks,
and 1 Month.

note When you create an Exchange account on your iPhone or iPod touch
and choose to sync contacts and calendars, any existing contact and
calendar information on the device is wiped out, replaced by contacts and
events from the Exchange server. Also, you can't synchronize this kind of data
with your computer via iTunes.

Configuring Web-based accounts

The iPhone's and iPod touch's designers made configuring one of these
accounts really easy. Just follow these steps:

1. Tap Settings > Mail, Contacts, Calendars.

2. Tap Add Account.

3. In the Add Account screen, choose your account type (Gmail, Yahoo, AOL, Hotmail, or MobileMe).

4. In the screen that appears next, enter your name, the email address for this account, your account's password, and a descriptive name for the account (*My Mighty MobileMe Account*, for example).

5. Tap Next.

Your account is verified, and then you're taken to a screen where you choose the information you'd like to sync with your device.

6. Set your sync options.

These options vary, depending on the features that each specific service offers. For a Yahoo account, for example, you can sync mail, contacts, calendars, reminders, and notes. For a regular Gmail account, you can sync only mail, calendars, and notes.

7. Tap Save.

Unlike its practice with other kinds of accounts, an iPhone or iPod touch doesn't demand settings for incoming and outgoing mail servers. It's intimately familiar with these services and does all that configuration for you. But you're welcome to muck with these more-arcane settings after you create the account, if you like (and I tell you how in the "Configuring further" section later in this chapter).

Configuring IMAP and POP accounts

Email accounts generally come in one of two flavors: IMAP (Internet Message Access Protocol) or POP (Post Office Protocol). Very loosely defined, with an IMAP account, your messages are stored on a server in the cloud. By contrast, although a POP account transfers messages from a server, those messages are stored locally on your computer. The iPhone and iPod touch support both kinds of accounts.

If you're like a lot of people and have an email account through a regular Internet service provider (ISP), such as one that provides email via a DSL or cable broadband connection, you'll configure your device this way:

1. Tap Settings > Mail, Contacts, Calendars.

2. Tap Add Account.

3. In the next screen, tap Other.

   I ask you to tap Other because this option lets you set up email accounts for ISPs other than those listed above the Other entry. In the resulting screen, you have the option to add mail accounts (as well as server-based contacts and calendars, which I deal with later in this chapter).

4. Tap Add Mail Account.

5. In the resulting New Account screen, enter the information for setting up a POP or IMAP account.

6. Tap Name, and enter your real name (as opposed to your user name).

7. Tap Address, and enter your email address (such as *example@ examplemail.com*).

8. Tap Password, and enter the account's password.

9. Tap Description, and enter a description of your account.

   I often use the name of my account for this entry—*Macworld*, for example.

10. Tap Next to verify your settings.

    The iPhone or iPod touch looks up the account settings you've entered. If you've set up an account for a common email carrier, such as Comcast or AT&T, it checks your account and configures the server settings for you.

If the device can't configure your account, or if the ISP offers IMAP and POP accounts and doesn't know which kind you have, the New Account screen displays new options.

11. Choose IMAP or POP.

At the top of the screen, you see IMAP and POP buttons. Tap the button for the kind of account you have.

12. Enter the host name in the Incoming Mail Server area.

This information, provided by your ISP, is in the format *mail. examplemail.com*.

13. Tap User Name, and enter the name that precedes the at (@) symbol in your email address.

If the address is *bruno@examplemail.com*, for example, type **bruno**.

tip On rare occasions, you need to enter the entire address in this field— *bruno@examplemail.com*, for example. If you receive an error message about the username or password, and everything else seems fine, try entering the entire address.

14. Tap Password, and enter the password for your email account.

15. Below Outgoing Mail Server, tap Host Name; then enter the appropriate text.

Once again, this text is provided by your ISP—typically in the format *smtp.examplemail.com*, though some services repeat the *mail. examplemail.com* format.

16. Enter your user name and password again, if required.

If these fields aren't filled in for you, copy this information from the Incoming Mail Server fields, and paste it here.

17. When you've double-checked to make sure everything's correct, tap Next in the top-right corner of the screen.

Your iPhone or iPod touch attempts to make a connection to your ISP, using the settings you entered. If it can't make a successful connection, it tells you so via a dialog box or two. To continue, you must enter settings that the device *will* accept. When you do, the device returns to the Mail, Contacts, Calendars screen, where the configured account appears in the list of accounts (**Figure 4.2**).

Figure 4.2
Configured POP email account.

Configuring further

Most people can stop right here and get on with mucking with Mail, but your email account may require a little extra tweaking for it to work. Here's how to do just that:

1. Tap Settings > Mail, Contacts, Calendars.

2. Tap your account name in the resulting screen, and if you'd like that account to appear in Mail's Accounts list, be sure that the Mail or Account slider is set to On.

tip Why turn it off instead? Perhaps you've got a load of messages sitting on the server that you'd rather not download on your iPhone or iPod touch. Download those messages on your computer instead, delete them from the server, and then enable the account on your device.

3. If the screen includes an Account field with your email address filled in, tap that account, and verify that the information in the account's settings fields is correct; if not, tap the field you want to edit, and start typing.

4. Tap the SMTP button to configure the outgoing server for your email account.

For details, see the sidebar "Out and About" later in this chapter.

5. Tap the Advanced button at the bottom of the screen.

6. In the resulting Advanced screen for POP accounts (**Figure 4.3**), choose the settings you want.

Figure 4.3
A POP account's Advanced settings.

Use these settings to specify the following:

- The interval that the device will wait before it removes deleted messages from the Trash (Never, After One Day, After One Week, or After One Month)

- Whether your account will use SSL protection to transmit and receive email

- The kind of authentication your account requires (Password, MD5 Challenge-Response, NTLM, or HTTP MD5 Digest)

- When you want email to be deleted from the server (Never, Seven Days, or When Removed from Inbox)

- The incoming server port for your account

- S/MIME setting (On or Off)

note   S/MIME is a security scheme for dealing with encrypted email that's new with iOS 5. If you intend to work with encrypted email, turn this setting on.

This information is individual enough that I'll leave it to your IT or ISP representative to tell you how to configure these options. Worth noting, however, is that you may be able to suss out these settings by looking at how the email client on your computer is configured.

For IMAP accounts, you have some different options in the Advanced window. You can choose which mailboxes will hold drafts, sent email, and deleted messages. You can choose when to remove deleted messages. You can also turn SSL on or off (except for Yahoo Mail, which doesn't offer an SSL option). You can choose the same authentication schemes as your POP-using sisters and brothers. You can enter an IMAP path prefix—a path name required by some IMAP servers so that they can show folders properly. As with POP accounts, you can also change the incoming server port.

Understanding Mail, Contacts, Calendars behavior

Before leaving the Mail, Contacts, Calendars screen, I'll cover the options that tell the Mail, Contacts, and Calendar applications how to behave.

View the bottom part of the screen, and you find these options (**Figure 4.4**):

Figure 4.4
Additional Mail settings.

Fetch New Data. New data such as events, contacts, notes, reminders, and email can be transferred (or *pushed*) to your iPhone or iPod touch automatically. You don't have to tell the device to retrieve this data; retrieval just happens. When you tap Fetch New Data, you're taken to the screen of the same name, where you can switch push off (**Figure 4.5**).

Additionally, you find Fetch settings here. Fetch is essentially a scheduler for your device; it tells the iPhone or iPod touch how often to go out and get information such as email messages from an account that can't push email, such as a POP account. (Fetch can also retrieve data from services such as iCloud and Yahoo that push data but for which you've turned push off.) You can configure the device to fetch data every 15 or 30 minutes, hourly, or manually.

Figure 4.5
The Fetch New Data screen.

If you tap the Advanced button at the bottom of the screen, you're taken to an Advanced screen, where you can determine how your various email accounts behave with regard to pushing and fetching. You can configure an iCloud or Yahoo account with a Push, Fetch, or Manual option, for example. Accounts such as Gmail that don't support push can be configured only for Fetch or Manual.

Show. How many messages would you like Mail to display? Options include 50, 100, 200, 500, and 1,000 recent messages.

Preview. When you view message subjects within a mailbox in one of your Mail accounts, you see the first bit of text in each message. The Preview entry determines how many lines of this text you see: none, 1, 2, 3, 4, or 5 lines.

Minimum Font Size. This setting determines the size of the text in your email messages: Small, Medium, Large, Extra Large, or Giant. (Medium is good for most eyes, and it saves a lot of scrolling.)

Show To/Cc Label. When this option is set to on, Mail plasters *To* next to messages that were sent directly to you and *Cc* next to messages on which you were copied.

Ask Before Deleting. When you switch this option on, if you tap the Trash icon to delete the message you're reading, you'll be asked to confirm your decision. If you swipe a message and then tap the red Delete button that appears or use the iPod touch's or iPhone's bulk-delete option, however, you won't be asked for confirmation.

Load Remote Images. Like the email client on your computer, the iPhone and iPod touch are capable of automatically showing you images embedded in messages. By default, this option is on. If you routinely retrieve mail over a slow Wi-Fi connection, however, consider turning this option off so that your device won't have to work to download the extra data.

Organize By Thread. The iPhone and iPod touch can organize email messages by thread. If you (or a group of people) engage in a back-and-forth email conversation with the local taxidermist, with all emails using the same Subject heading, and this option is switched on, you'll see a single entry for that conversation in your inbox. A number on the right side of that entry indicates how many messages are part of the thread.

Always Bcc Myself. If you're the kind of person who wants a copy of every message you send (but don't want the recipients of those messages to know), switch this option on. You'll get your copies.

Increase Quote Level. Increase Quote Level is another new feature introduced with iOS 5. When this option is switched on, any copied text in a message that you forward or reply to is indented, with a small vertical line placed before it.

Signature. Ever wonder where that proud *Sent from My iPhone/iPod* message comes from—the one that appears at the bottom of every message you send from your device? Right here. As a new iPhone or iPod touch owner, you'll want to stick with this default message for a while, simply for the bragging rights. When the novelty has worn off, feel free to tap this option and enter some pithy signoff of your own.

Default Account. If you have more than one email account set up, this setting determines which account will send photos, videos, notes, and YouTube links. When you send one of these items, you can't choose which account sends it, so give this option some thought. You may discover that Wi-Fi hotspots are reluctant to send mail through your regular ISP's SMTP server, whereas Gmail accounts rarely have this problem. For this reason, you may want to make your Gmail account the default.

The Contacts settings shown in **Figure 4.6** appear next:

Figure 4.6
*Additional
Contacts and
Calendar settings.*

Sort Order. Tap this option to choose between sorting contacts by First, Last name or by Last, First name.

Display Order. Similar to Sort Order, this option lets you display your contacts as either First, Last or Last, First.

My Info. This is your contact information, selected from the Contacts app. When an app wants to access or send this information, this contact is the one it goes to.

Default Account (iPhone only). If you create a new contact that's not specifically tied to a particular account, that contact is added to the account listed here—your Gmail account, for example.

Import SIM Contacts (iPhone only). If you've inserted a SIM card from another iPhone that contains contacts, you can use this command to import them. Tap this button, and you see a list of accounts that support importing contacts.

Next are the Calendar settings (refer to Figure 4.6):

New Invitation Alerts. This On/Off switch lets you view—or not— meeting invitations you've received (those pushed to you from an Exchange server, for example).

Sync. This option lets you choose a range of past events to sync with your device. Choices include Events 2 Weeks Back, 1 Month Back, 3 Months Back, 6 Months Back, and All Events.

Time Zone Support. Tap this command, and you're taken to the Time Zone Support screen, where you can turn Time Zone Support on or off. Below that setting, choose the time zone of a major city.

When Time Zone Support is on, Calendar's events are shown in the time of the selected city. So, for example, you could choose London even if you're in San Francisco and see events in London time. Switch this option off, and events are shown in the device's current location (which is configured in the Date & Time setting).

Default Alert Times. Using this setting, you can create a default time for alerts to go off before a birthday event, single event, or all-day event. You might tap Events and choose 1 Hour Before from the resulting Events screen. Now, whenever you create a new event, by default an alert goes off an hour before the event takes place. This setting is simply a global shortcut; you're welcome to change it whenever you create a new event. (I talk about creating events later in this chapter.)

Default Calendar. Tap this command to choose a calendar where the iPhone or iPod touch will add events created outside the Calendar app.

Finally, at the bottom of the screen is the Reminders section (**Figure 4.7**). The options in this section, like the Reminders app itself, are new to iOS 5:

Figure 4.7
You'll find Reminders' settings at the bottom of the Mail, Contacts, Calendars screen.

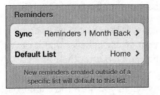

Reminders	
Sync	Reminders 1 Month Back >
Default List	Home >

New reminders created outside of a specific list will default to this list.

Sync. This simple setting allows you to choose how far back reminders will be synced. Your options include 2 weeks, 1 month, 3 months, 6 months, and all reminders.

Default List. Similar to Default Account and Default Calendar, Default List is where you select the account that will receive events created outside the Reminders app.

Out and About

iOS is very smart about sending email. It works like this:

In the old days, you configured your email account with a particular SMTP server. If you took your iPhone or iPod touch on the road, and that SMTP server didn't work, you were stuck with an email message in the outbox that wouldn't send. This problem usually happened because of an antispam measure: The network you were connected to (in a coffee shop or hotel, for example) didn't allow messages to be relayed from one ISP's SMTP server through another's SMTP server.

You can work around this situation with your iPhone and iPod touch. Just select an account in the Mail, Contacts, Calendars screen; tap the account name in the resulting screen if necessary; and tap the SMTP button. You see a list of all the SMTP servers your device has settings for. At the top of the list is the primary server—the server address you entered (or that was entered for you) when you created the account. Next to this server's name is the word **On**.

Below the primary server is the Other SMTP Servers entry, listing all other SMTP servers your device believes that it can access. By default, these entries have the word **Off** after their names. Tap one (a Gmail server, for example), and in the resulting screen, you have the option to turn that server on. When you do, if the iPhone or iPod touch is prevented from sending messages from the primary server, it tries to send from one of the other servers that you've enabled.

This feature alone justifies getting a free iCloud, Gmail, or Yahoo account, as public Wi-Fi hotspots rarely block mail sent through these services' SMTP servers.

(Continues on next page)

Out and About (continued)

I'll mention one other SMTP option while I'm here: If you need to change the SMTP server port from the default setting, you do it by tapping an SMTP server in the SMTP screen, tapping the Server Port entry at the bottom of the screen, and then typing a new value on the onscreen numeric keyboard that appears. Why do it? Many ISPs provide an SMTP server port (usually, 587) that can be relayed through other SMTP servers. If you find that your device can't send a message, try changing your email account's SMTP port to 587 or to the public port number provided by your ISP.

Sending and Receiving Mail

Now that your accounts are *finally* set up properly, you can send and receive messages. The process works this way.

Receiving email

Receiving email is dead simple. Just follow these steps:

1. Tap the Mail icon in the iPhone's or iPod touch's Home screen.

   Mail checks for new messages when you first launch the application. If you have new messages, the device downloads them.

   When you launch the Mail app, by default you see the Mailboxes screen (**Figure 4.8**), which contains two sections: Inboxes and Accounts. In the Inboxes section, you see all the email accounts set up on your iPhone or iPod touch, plus the All Inboxes entry, which lets you view all received messages regardless of the accounts they were received from. The Accounts section also lists all email accounts on your device. Next to each entry in both areas is a number that indicates the number of unread messages—*Gmail 18*, for example.

Figure 4.8
The Mail app's Mailboxes screen.

2. Tap All Inboxes or an account name in the Inboxes section.

If you tap one of the items in the Inboxes section, you'll be taken to an Inbox screen that displays all the messages in that account's inbox. Messages appear in a list, with the most recently received messages at the top. Unread messages have a blue dot next to them. Messages with attachments bear a paper-clip icon. Threaded messages display a number indicating the number of messages that make up the thread. Finally, the Inbox heading has a number in parentheses next to it—*Inbox (22)*, for example. That *(22)* means that you have 22 unread messages.

This screen also bears a Compose icon in the bottom-right corner and a Retrieve icon in the bottom-left corner. Tap Retrieve to check for new mail.

An Edit button in the top-right corner of the All Inboxes screen lets you delete, move, or mark messages. Tap it, and all the messages in the list acquire a dim gray circle, which marks messages that you want to delete, move, or mark. Tap one of these circles, and a red check icon appears within it. Continue tapping messages until you've selected all the messages you'd like to delete, move, or mark; then tap the Delete button at the bottom of the screen. All the messages you selected move to the Trash.

tip   Alternatively, with regard to deleting messages, you can do without the Edit button. Swipe your finger across a message entry to force a Delete button to appear, and tap Delete. The message moves to the Trash.

note   You say you see the word *Archive* instead of *Delete*? That's because you're doing this with a Gmail account. With Gmail accounts, you send "deleted" items to your Gmail archive rather than to the Trash.

Tap Move, and a Mailboxes sheet scrolls up from the bottom, listing all available mailboxes for that account. Choose a mailbox, and the selected messages move to it. This move feature is really useful only if you're using an IMAP account, as unlike POP accounts, IMAP accounts can have additional folders for filing email messages.

Finally, when you select messages and tap Mark, you're offered the option to flag the messages or mark them as read. When you flag messages, a small orange flag appears next to the messages' text preview, indicating that the message is marked. Tapping Mark As Read does exactly that. To unflag a message, just tap Edit, tap the gray circle next to it, and tap Mark again; then tap Unflag in the resulting sheet.

3. Tap an account name in the Accounts area.

You see all the mailboxes that make up that account. For POP accounts, those mailboxes include Inbox, Drafts (if you've saved any composed messages without sending them), Sent (if you've sent any messages from that account), and Trash (if you've deleted any messages from that account). For IMAP accounts, you'll most likely see Inbox, Drafts,

Sent, Trash, and any folders associated with the account—folders that you've added to an iCloud or Gmail account, for example.

These folder names, however, depend entirely on what the host service calls them. Gmail, for example, gathers the messages you've sent in the Sent Mail folder (**Figure 4.9**).

Figure 4.9
A Gmail account screen.

Really Deleting a Message

When you delete or archive a message, it's not really gone; it's simply moved to the Trash or Archive mailbox. To delete the message for real, you can either wait out the remove interval listed in the account's Mail setting (see "Configuring further" earlier in this chapter) or tap Trash. Then you can swipe a message and tap the Delete button that appears next to the message; tap Edit and then tap Delete All at the bottom of the screen; or cherry-pick the messages you want to delete by tapping the gray circles next to them and then tapping the Delete (#) button (where # equals the number of messages you've selected). Then—and only then—is a message truly gone. As for archived messages, select the archive mailbox, tap Edit, select the messages you want to delete, and tap Delete (#) at the bottom of the screen.

New with iOS 5 is the ability to create new mailboxes on an iOS device. To do that, just tap an IMAP account in the Accounts list (such as a Gmail account); tap the Edit button in the top-right corner of the device's screen; and then tap the New Mailbox button in the bottom-right corner of the screen. In the Edit Mailbox screen that appears, name your new mailbox, and choose a location for it by tapping the Mailbox Location field. Tap Save when you're done.

In the bottom-right corner of an account screen, you see a Compose icon. Tap it, and a New Message screen appears, along with the iPhone's or iPod touch's keyboard. I talk about creating new messages in "Creating and sending email" later in this chapter.

Spam and iOS Devices

As I write these words, the Mail application lacks a spam filter—a utility that looks through your incoming email for junk mail and quarantines it in a special mailbox. This lack is a drag if you're using an account that attracts a lot of spam.

My solution? Don't use such an account on your device. Google offers its free Gmail email service at www.gmail.com. Gmail provides loads of email storage (probably more than your current ISP does), and you can access it from the Web, your iOS device, and your computer's email client. Best of all, it offers excellent spam filtering.

Additionally, you can set up Gmail so that your other POP mail accounts are forwarded to it. This setup allows Gmail to filter out spam from these accounts, too, before the mail is delivered to your inbox.

Like I said, Gmail is free. Give it a try.

Navigating the Message screen

Simple though it may be, the Message screen packs a punch. In it, you find not only standard email elements such as From and To fields, Subject, and message body, but also icons for adding contacts and for filing, trashing, replying to, and forwarding messages. The screen breaks down this way.

Before the body

The top of the Message screen displays the number of messages in the mailbox as well as the number of the displayed message—*2 of 25*, for example. Tap the up or down arrow to the right to move quickly to the previous or next message in the mailbox (**Figure 4.10**).

Figure 4.10
Message body with document attached.

Below that, you see From and To fields. Each field displays at least one contact name or email address (one of which could be your own) in a blue bubble. Tap one of these bubbles, and if the name or address is in your device's Contacts directory, you're taken to its owner's Info screen. If the name or address isn't among your contacts, a new screen appears, offering you the option of emailing the person, creating a new contact, or adding the address to an existing Contacts entry (**Figure 4.11**). By now, if you've been following along, you understand how to create a new contact as well as edit an existing contact.

Figure 4.11
An unknown contact's Info screen.

You can hide the To field by tapping the Hide entry near it. This action hides all the To fields in all the messages in all your accounts, and it changes the Hide entry to Details. To expose the To fields again, just tap Details.

Below the From and To fields is the message subject, followed by the date. If you have details showing, you also see a Mark entry. Tap this entry, and you can choose to flag it or mark it as unread.

Body talk

Finally, in the body area of the message, are the pithy words you've been waiting for. Just as in your computer's email client, you see the text of the message in this area. Quoted text appears with a vertical line to its left —or more than one line, depending on how many quote layers the message has. If a message has several quote layers, each layer is a different color.

If the message has attachments, they appear below the message text (**Figure 4.12**). When Cousin Bill sends you a photo from his latest vacation, for example, it appears here.

Figure 4.12
Message with attached photo.

Retrieve   Trash/   Compose
           Archive

     Mailboxes   Send

URLs, email addresses, and phone numbers contained within messages appear as live blue hyperlinks. Tap a URL, and Safari launches and takes you to that Web page. Tap an email address, and a new email message opens with that address in the To field. On the iPhone, a tapped phone number fires up the Phone app so you can call that number. On the iPod touch, tapping a phone number causes a sheet to appear; in it, you see the options Create New Account and Add to Existing Contact.

The tools below

The toolbar at the bottom of the screen contains five icons (refer to Figure 5.12):

Retrieve. Tap this circular icon, and the device checks for new messages in that account.

Mailboxes. When you tap the Mailboxes icon, you're presented with a list of all the mailboxes associated with that account. Tap one of these mailboxes, and the message is filed there. (This method is one way to move items out of the Trash, though the Trash screen also includes a Move button.)

Trash/Archive. Again, whether you see a Trash or Archive icon depends on the kind of account you're using. A POP account shows a Trash icon, whereas most IMAP accounts offer an Archive icon. Tap this icon to toss the message in the Trash or file it in an archive.

Send. The left-arrow icon is your pathway to the Reply, Reply All, Forward, Save Image, Print, and Cancel commands (**Figure 4.13**). It's unlikely that you'll see all these options in one sheet, because the items that appear depend on the number of recipients and on whether an image is attached.

Figure 4.13
The Reply sheet.

When you tap the Send icon and then the Reply button in the resulting sheet, a new message appears, with the Subject heading *Re: Original Message Subject*, in which *Original Message Sub*ject is...well, you know. The message is addressed to the sender of the original message, and the insertion point awaits at the top of the message body. The original text is quoted below. The message is mailed from the account you're working in.

If a message you received was sent to multiple recipients, tapping Reply All lets you reply to all the recipients of the original message.

Tap Forward, and you're responsible for filling in the To field in the resulting message. You can type it yourself with the keyboard that appears or tap the plus (+) icon to add a recipient from your device's list of contacts. This message bears *Fwd:* at the beginning of the Subject heading, followed by the original heading. The original message's From and To fields appear at the top of the message as quoted text followed by the original message.

If a message has images attached to it, you see a Save *x* Images button, where *x* is the number of images. (The button reads Save Image if there's just one image.) Tap that button, and the images are added to the Camera Roll collection in the Photos application.

Devices running iOS 5 are capable of printing to compatible wireless printers (see Chapter 10 for sneakier ways). If you have such a printer, tap Print to print the message.

Compose. Last is your old friend the Compose icon. Tap it, and a New Message screen appears, ready for your input.

Creating and sending email

If it truly is better to give than receive, the following instructions for composing and delivering mail from your iPhone or iPod touch should enrich your life significantly. With regard to email, these devices can give nearly as good as they get. Here's how to go about it.

As I mention earlier in the chapter, you can create new email messages by tapping the Compose icon that appears in every account and mailbox screen. To create a message, follow these steps:

1. Tap the Compose icon.

By default, Mail fills the From field with the address for this account. (If you tap the Compose icon in the Mailboxes screen, the message is sent from the account selected as the default account in the Mail, Contacts, Calendars screen.) But you needn't use that account. Just tap From, and any other email accounts you have appear in a scrolling list. Tap the one you want.

2. In the New Message screen that appears, type the recipient's email address; tap the plus icon next to the To field; or, if you have an iPhone 4S, tap the Microphone button and say the name of the person you want to send the message to.

When you place the insertion point in the To or Cc/Bcc field, notice that the iPhone's or iPod touch's keyboard adds @ and period (.) characters where the spacebar usually resides. (The spacebar is still there; it's just smaller.) This feature makes typing addresses easier because you don't have to switch to the numbers-and-symbols keyboard.

 tip Tap and hold the period key, and .net, .edu, .org, .us, and .com pop up as part of a contextual menu. How handy is that?

When you start typing a name, the device suggests recipients based on entries in your list of contacts (**Figure 4.14**). If the recipient you want appears in the list below the To field, tap that name to add it to the field.

Figure 4.14
Begin typing to find a contact.

When you tap the plus icon, your list of contacts appears. Navigate through your contacts, and tap the one you want to add to the To field. Some contacts may have multiple email addresses; tap the one you'd like to use. To add more names to the To field, type them or tap the plus icon to add them.

To delete a recipient, tap that person's address and then tap the Delete key on the device's keyboard.

tip With iOS 5, you can rearrange the order of contacts you place in the To field. To do that, just tap a contact's name and drag it to a new position. Other contacts move out of the way to accommodate the one you've dragged.

3. If you'd like to Cc or Bcc someone, tap the appropriate field (Cc or Bcc) and then use any of the techniques in step 2 to add the recipient.

4. Tap the Subject field, and enter a subject for your message with the keyboard (or a Bluetooth keyboard, if you've configured the device to use one).

That subject replaces *New Message* at the top of the screen.

5. Tap inside the message body (or, if the insertion point is in the Subject field, tap Return on the keyboard to move to the message body), and type your message—or, if you have an iPhone 4, dictate the message by tapping the Microphone button, speaking, and then tapping Done.

6. Format your text, if you want.

Another new iOS 5 feature is the ability to format your text (lightly). Just select some text in the message body, using the technique I outline in Chapter 1, and in the bubble that appears, tap the right-pointing triangle. Then tap the BIU icon and choose Bold, Italics, or Underline to format the text exactly that way.

> **tip** While you're playing with this bubble, note that you can place your cursor in a line of text, tap the right-pointing arrow, and view a Quote Level command. Tap it and then choose Decrease or Increase to change the text's quote level.

7. Tap Send to send the message or Cancel to save or delete your message.

The Send icon, in the top-right corner, is easy enough to understand. Tap that icon, and the message is sent from the current account. You'll know that it's been sent when you hear a swoosh sound (unless you've switched off the Sent Mail sound in the Sounds setting, of course).

Cancel is a little more confusing. If you've typed anywhere in the To field, the New Message screen's Subject field, or the message body (even if you subsequently deleted everything you typed), a sheet rolls up when you tap Cancel, displaying Delete Draft, Save Draft, and Cancel buttons. Tap Delete Draft to do just that. Tap Save Draft to store the message in the account's Drafts mailbox. (If no such mailbox exists, the iPhone or iPod touch creates one.) If you tap Cancel, the device assumes that you made a mistake when you tapped Cancel the first time, and it removes this sheet.

If the device can't send a message—when you don't have access to a Wi-Fi network, for example—it creates an outbox for the account from which you're trying to send the message. When you next use Mail and are able to send the message, the iPhone or iPod touch makes the connection and sends any messages in the outbox, at which point the outbox disappears.

Using Calendar

In the old days, the only ways to get events on an iPhone's or iPod touch's calendar were to type them on the device or to sync the device with iTunes and ask it to copy your events from the computer to the iPhone or iPod touch. Thanks to the cloud-based push synchronization that's common today, however, the Calendar app is a smarter application than it once was. In this section, I take a look at all the ways you can put life's events on your iPhone or iPod touch.

Managing many calendars

When you launch the Calendar app, by default you see a page displaying the current month, with the current day highlighted. When you tap the Calendars icon in the top-left corner, you're whisked to the Calendars screen, where you can switch calendars on and off.

That's right—much like Mail's unified inbox, the Calendar app's unified calendar shows events from all those calendars you've enabled. So if you want to view just the events on your Work calendar, enable just that calendar. (A calendar is enabled when it has a check mark next to its name in the Calendars screen.) The Calendars screen also displays any calendars synced from the cloud—from Google, Yahoo, and iCloud, for example. You can turn these calendars off as well. To return to calendar view, tap Done in the top-right corner of the screen.

Viewing events

Calendar is capable of displaying events in three views: Month, Day, and List. They're laid out like so.

Month

As I mention earlier, when you launch Calendar, you see this month's calendar by default, with today's date highlighted in blue. Other days maintain a gray, businesslike appearance. Tap another day, and it adopts the blue box, while the present day gains a deeper gray hue. To return to the current day, tap it (if you're viewing the current month), or tap the Today button in the bottom-left corner of the screen. To move to the previous or next month, tap the Previous or Next arrow beside the month heading. To scan backward and forward faster, tap and hold one of these arrows.

Any days on the calendar that have events appended to them bear a small black dot below the date. Tap a day with a dot, and the events for that day appear in a list below the calendar (**Figure 4.15**), each preceded by its start time and a colored dot indicating the calendar to which the event is attached. (Calendars are color-coded.) Tap an event in this list, and you're taken to the Event screen, which details the name and location of the event, its date, its start and end times, any alerts you've created, and any notes you've added for the event.

Figure 4.15
A day in Month view with two events.

To edit or delete the event, tap the Edit icon in the top-right corner of the screen. Within the Edit screen, tap one of the fields to change its information. (I discuss these fields in "Creating events" later in this chapter.) To delete an event, tap the red Delete Event button at the bottom of the screen; then tap the Delete Event confirmation icon that appears.

Day

Tap the Day view button, and as you'd expect, you see the day laid out in a list, divided into hours. The day of the week and its date appear near the top of the screen. To move to the previous or next day, tap the Previous or Next arrow. To scan backward or forward more quickly, tap and hold the appropriate arrow.

Each event appears as a colored bar (again, each calendar is color-coded, and that coding is reflected here) spanning the time that the event occupies and labeled with the name of the appointment and its location (**Figure 4.16**). All-day events appear just below the day and date near the top of the screen. Just as you do with events in Month view, tap them to reveal their details; to edit them, tap the Edit button.

Figure 4.16
*A day in Day view
with two events.*

List

List view shows a list of all the events on your calendar, separated by gray date bars. Each gray bar bears the day's abbreviated name (*Fri* or *Mon*, for example) and the month, date, and year of the event. The event's title appears just below, preceded by its start time and a colored dot indicating its calendar association. Once again, tap an event to view its details. Tap Edit to edit the event or delete it via the Delete Event button (**Figure 4.17**).

Creating events

Creating events on the iPhone and iPod touch is simple. Just tap the plus icon in the top-right corner of the screen to produce the Add Event screen, where you'll find a list of fields:

- **Title, Location.** The title of the event appears when you select the event's date in Month view. Both an event's title and location appear in the Day-view list, and in List view, you see just the event's title. As with any other field on the iPod touch or iPhone, just type the entries, and tap Save when you're done.

- **Starts/Ends/Time Zone.** The title is explanation enough. Just tap the Starts/ Ends field, and in the resulting Start & End

Figure 4.17
Editing an event.

screen, enter a start date and time by using the spinning wheels at the bottom (**Figure 4.18**). Then tap the Ends field, and dial in an end date and time. If the event lasts all day, tap the All-Day switch to set it to On. Finally, tap the Time Zone field, and in the screen that appears, enter a city within the time zone you want to use (San Francisco for Pacific time, for example).

Figure 4.18
*Set the duration
of your event.*

- **Repeat.** You can create an event that occurs every day, week, 2 weeks, month, or year. This method is a convenient way to remind yourself of your kid's weekly piano lesson or your own wedding anniversary.

- **Invitees.** With iOS 5, you can associate contacts with your events. Just tap Invitees, and in the screen that appears, tap the plus icon to add contacts to your event.

- **Alert.** A fat lot of good an electronic calendar does you if you're not paying attention to the date or time. Tap Alert, and direct the device to sound an alert at a specific time before the event's start (5, 15, or 30 minutes; 1 or 2 hours; or 1 or 2 days) or on the day of the event.

  You can create two alerts per event—useful when you want to remind yourself of events for the day and need another mental nudge a few minutes before the event occurs. Also, as I mention earlier in the chapter, you can create a default interval for alerts to sound within the Mail, Contacts, Calendars setting.

- **Calendar.** Using this command, you can assign the new event to any calendar you have on your device.

- **Availability.** Tap this entry to choose to designate yourself as busy or free.

- **URL.** Add an associated URL here (such as the Google Maps location of your meeting).

- **Notes.** Feel free to type a bit of text to remind yourself exactly why you're allowing Bob Whosis to dominate your Thursday afternoon.

Syncing events

Your computer and your iPhone or iPod touch have a nice sharing relationship with regard to events. When you create an event on one device, it's copied to the other, complete with title, location, start and end times, alerts (likely called *alarms* in your computer's calendar program), and notes.

As I explain in Chapter 2, iTunes' Info tab lets you choose the computer-based calendars that you want to sync with the device. If you have an Exchange, Gmail, Yahoo, or iCloud account, calendar events associated with those accounts are pushed to your device (and the device pushes right back those events that you create on it).

Subscribing to a calendar

You can also subscribe to Web-based calendars with your iPhone or iPod touch, which supports both CalDAV and iCal formats. To do so, follow these steps:

1. Tap Settings > Mail, Contacts, Calendars > Add Account.

2. Tap Other in the Add Account screen.

3. In the Calendars section of the Other screen, choose either Add CalDAV Account or Add Subscribed Calendar.

Which option you choose depends on the kind of calendar you want to subscribe to. iCal calendars are generally available to the public and require only that you have a server address in the form *example.com/ example.ics*. CalDAV calendars are server-based; they require you to know the name of the host server and to have a user name and password for that server.

4. Enter the required information to subscribe to the calendar.

Getting Reminders

Capable and generally feature-complete though the iPhone and iPod touch were before iOS 5, they were incapable of creating and syncing to-do items—those little nag notes you create that pop up every so often to let you know the many ways in which you've failed to accomplish your goals. Apple rectified this situation in iOS 5 with the Reminders app. Here's how it works.

Creating a reminder

To create a reminder, follow these steps:

1. Tap the Reminders icon on the iPhone's or iPod touch's Home screen.

You see an empty Reminders page.

2. Tap the Lists button in the top-left corner, choose the calendar you want to associate your reminder with, and then tap Done.

You may have just a single calendar or multiple calendars scattered across several email accounts.

3. Tap the plus icon.

The device's onscreen keyboard appears.

4. Enter a short reminder along the lines of "Finish the book" (**Figure 4.19**).

Figure 4.19
Adding a reminder.

5. Tap the keyboard's Return key if you want to create another reminder.

6. Repeat steps 3–5 for all the reminders you want to create.

7. When you're finished, tap Done.

8. Tap one of the reminders you've created to open the detail screen.

9. Tap Remind Me.

The Remind Me screen that you see next depends on whether you have an iPhone or an iPod touch:

- *If you have an iPod,* you see a single On a Day entry. Flick the switch to On, and a date field appears, displaying the current date and time. Tap that field and use the scroll wheels to choose a different day and/or time. When that moment in time arrives, you receive an alert on your device.

- *If you have an iPhone,* you see both On a Day and an additional entry: At a Location (**Figure 4.20**). Flick the latter entry's switch to On, and you can choose to set a location by selecting one associated with a contact, such as your sister-in-law's house or the local juke joint. Then you can choose to have an alert go off when you leave or when you arrive.

Figure 4.20
The Remind Me screen on an iPhone.

The scenario works this way: You've created a reminder called Buy Rabbit Food and associated Judy's Pet Supply with it as the location (because you've created a contact for Judy and her shop). You've chosen to have an alert go off when you arrive. Sure enough, the following Sunday, you're at the mall to pick up a coffee, and because the café is next to Judy's, the alert goes off, reminding you to get food for the bunnies.

10. When you complete a task, simply tap the empty check box next to it.

11. To delete a task, tap it, and in the resulting screen, tap the Delete button.

Viewing reminders

You can view reminders as a list of all reminders associated with a particular calendar, as well as by date. You do this via either the List or Date button. When you tap List, you can swipe through the various calendars

you've associated with your reminders. The first calendar is always
Completed (**Figure 4.21**). Swipe to the left to march through calendars.

Figure 4.21
*The Completed
reminders screen.*

Tap the Date button, and the reminders associated with a particular date
appear. Remember that reminders appear on the days when they were
created, not on the days they're due. To move through dates, you can
swipe to the left to move forward or to the right to travel back, or tap the
arrow keys at the bottom of the screen. To view today's reminders, just
tap Today.

 If you find navigating this way to be slow going, tap the Calendar icon
in the top-left corner to view a calendar presented in Month view.

To search for a reminder, you can tap the Calendars icon when viewing
reminders in Date view or tap the Lists button when viewing them as
lists. Each screen has a Search Reminders field at the top of the screen.
Just tap that field and use the device's keyboard to enter a search term.
As you type, any matching results appear in the Search window.

Syncing and organizing reminders

What makes the Reminders app particularly useful is that it syncs with cloud-based services, including iCloud. This means that if you add a reminder to your iPhone or iPod touch and have configured Reminders to be synced, any tasks that you create on your device are also synced with iCal on your Mac or Outlook on your Windows PC. Likewise, create a reminder in one of these applications on your computer, and that reminder is synced to your iOS device.

5

Safari

From Day One, the iPhone and iPod touch have had a real live Web browser, very much like the one on your computer. In this chapter, I show you how to use it to best advantage. Let's go surfing!

Syncing Bookmarks

I know you're eager to start surfing the Web with Safari, but you'll find the experience far more pleasant if you first sync your Safari (Mac) or Safari or Internet Explorer (Windows) bookmarks to your device. You have a couple of ways to do this. The easiest is to sync your bookmarks and data through iCloud, as I explain in Chapter 2. If you prefer to do things the old-fashioned way through iTunes, simply plug in your iPhone or iPod touch, select it in iTunes' Source list, click the Info tab, enable the Safari or Internet Explorer option, and sync the device.

Surfin' Safari

When you first tap the Safari icon at the bottom of the iPhone's or iPod touch's Home screen, you may be surprised to see a full (though tiny) representation of a Web page appear before your eyes. Safari on the iPhone and iPod touch is nearly the real deal. (In "Seeing Safari's limits" later in this chapter, I talk about how that isn't quite the case.)

At first glance, though, it's the real *small* deal. The pages Safari displays on these devices are Lilliputian at first, but you have ways to make these pages legible:

- **Turn the device on its side.** Yes, Safari, like nearly all the included apps, works in both portrait and landscape orientation. It displays the entire width of a Web page in either view, so when you switch to landscape orientation, you see more detail as the page enlarges to fill the device's screen (**Figure 5.2**).

Figure 5.2
A Web page in landscape orientation, showing Safari's tools.

- **Stretch the page open.** You can enlarge the page by using the stretch gesture (see Chapter 1). When the page is enlarged, tap and drag to reposition it.

- **Double-tap a column.** Most Web pages include columns of text and graphics. To zoom in on a single column, double-tap it. That column expands to fill the device's screen. To shrink the page to its original size, double-tap the screen again.

- **Double-tap part of the page.** If a Web page lacks columns, you can still zoom in by double-tapping the page.

Browsing the Web

Like any good browser, Safari provides numerous ways to get around the Web. Let me count the ways.

Getting addressed

Like your computer's Web browser, Safari has an Address field at the top of its main window. (If you don't see the Address field, just tap the gray menu bar at the top of the screen, and you'll be taken to the top of the page, where the Address field is revealed.) To travel to a Web site, tap in this field. When you do, the keyboard appears. If ever there were an argument for using Safari in landscape orientation, this feature is it, because the keyboard is far less cramped this way (**Figure 5.3**).

Figure 5.3
The landscape Safari keyboard (with the .com key held down).

Type the Web address you want to visit. The iPhone or iPod touch and its keyboard make this process as easy for you as possible. To begin with, you needn't type *http://www*. Safari understands that just about every Web address begins this way and doesn't require you to type the prefix. Just type *examplesite*; then tap the .com key at the bottom of the keyboard (even .com is unnecessary sometimes), and tap Go. In a short time, the page you desire appears.

> **tip** If a site's URL ends with something like .net or .org, you needn't key it in. Just tap and hold the keyboard's .com entry until a pop-up menu appears, offering additional .net, .edu, .org, and .us entries. Glide your finger over to the entry you want, and let go. The address autocompletes with the extension you chose.

Safari offers some other convenient shortcuts for entering addresses. If you've visited the site before, for example, it's likely to be in Safari's History list. If so, just begin typing the address or a keyword in that address, and it appears below the Address field (**Figure 5.4**). Tap the address to go to that Web site.

Figure 5.4
The History list can save typing.

If you need to type a more complex address—*example.com/pictures/ vacation.html*, for example—the default keyboard for Safari can help, because it includes both period (.) and slash (/) keys.

To leave the keyboard behind without doing anything, tap the Cancel button. If the page you're trying to visit is taking too long to load, or if you've changed your mind about visiting it, just tap the X that appears at the right end of the Address field while the page is loading. Safari will stop loading the page. If you'd like to reload a page that's fully loaded, tap the Reload icon next to the Address field (the one that takes the place of the X when a page is completely loaded).

Searching

You can also conduct Google, Yahoo, or Bing searches from the keyboard. To begin a search, just tap the magnifying-glass icon in the top-left corner of a Safari window. This tap causes the keyboard to appear and the insertion point to blink in the Search field. Enter your query in this field and then tap Google, Yahoo, or Bing (depending on which search engine you're using).

By default, the iPhone and iPod touch use Google search. To switch to Yahoo or Bing, tap Settings > Safari > Search Engine and then tap the search engine you'd like to use.

You can also search the contents of a page. To do that, tap the Search field, and enter the word or phrase you're looking for. At the bottom of the screen, you'll see *On This Page (X Matches)*, where *X* is the number of matching items on the page. Tap *Find "nameofitem,"* and Safari will high-light every instance of the item you're looking for in yellow.

Navigating with links

Links work just as they do in your computer's browser. Just tap a link to go to the associated Web page. Two things are worth noting:

- Safari is sometimes reluctant to use a link while it's still loading a Web page. To speed things up, tap the X icon at the right end of the Address field to stop the current page from loading; then tap the link to load its target immediately. (In some cases, you'll see a blank page instead of the page you were on, because Safari had started to load the new page but hadn't completed the process. In such cases, tap the Back icon to return to the previous page.)

- When you hover your mouse pointer over a link in your computer's Web browser, you can view information about where that link will take you. The iPhone and iPod touch offer a more powerful, though hidden, capability. Just tap and hold a link, and a sheet scrolls up from the bottom. This sheet displays not only the full address of the link, but also five options—Open, Open in New Page, Add to Reading List, Copy, and Cancel—whose names match their purposes (**Figure 5.5**).

Figure 5.5
Tap and hold a link to see these options.

Going back and forward

Just like your computer's Web browser, Safari has Back and Forward icons for moving through sites you've visited.

Check out Reading List

Reading List is a new feature introduced with iOS 5 (and also a feature of Apple's Web browser, Safari 5.1). Reading List is similar to a bookmark repository. As a matter of fact, you access Reading List from within the Bookmarks screen by tapping the Bookmarks icon at the bottom of the Safari screen. Tap Reading List, and you see a list of Web pages that you've saved. You can view all the saved pages by tapping the All button at the top of the list or just view those you haven't read by tapping Unread. To read an associated page, just tap it.

How is this feature different from a standard bookmark? Other than the All and Unread entries, you see a small icon that represents the site, along with a headline and some preview text. Bookmarks show you only the name of the Web page.

Items in your Reading List aren't stored on your iPhone or iPod touch; they're just links to these pages. If you want to read the full page, you must be able to get to the Internet via a Wi-Fi or cellular connection.

Saving pages

In the bottom-right corner of the Safari screen, you see a small Pages icon. Tap it, and you see a small representation of the page you're currently viewing. Tap the New Page button in the bottom-left corner of the screen, and you can create a new empty Web page, saving the page you were just viewing in the process (**Figure 5.6**). This feature is the device's equivalent of browser tabs.

Figure 5.6
Safari lets you save up to eight pages.

You can repeat this process to save as many as eight pages; the Pages icon displays the number of pages you've stored. To visit one of your saved pages, tap the Pages icon, and flick your finger across the display to move back or forward through the saved pages. To view a page full-screen, tap its thumbnail or tap the Done button while its thumbnail is on view. To delete a page, tap the X in the top-left corner of the page.

note The contents of saved pages aren't cached to the iPhone or iPod touch—just their locations—so you won't be able to read them if your device is offline (when you can't access a Wi-Fi network, for example).

Navigating with bookmarks

You heeded my advice to sync or import your computer browser's bookmarks, right? Great. Bookmarks are another fine way to get where you want to go.

Just tap the Bookmarks icon at the bottom of Safari's screen. The Bookmarks screen appears, replete with your bookmarks organized as they were on your computer the last time you synced your device. By this, I mean that if you've organized your computer's bookmarks in folders, that's just how they'll appear on your iPhone or iPod touch. Bookmarks that you've placed in Safari's Bookmarks bar are contained in their own folder, named (aptly enough) Bookmarks Bar. Reading List, which I mention in a sidebar earlier in this chapter, appears at the top of the list.

Tap a folder to view the bookmarks it contains. To travel to a bookmark's target page, tap the bookmark.

Working with bookmarks

Bookmarks are important-enough components of Safari that they deserve more than this so-far-brief mention. How, for example, do you create bookmarks, organize and edit the ones you have, and delete those you no longer need? Like this.

Creating bookmarks

You've found a Web site you like while surfing with the iPhone or iPod touch. To bookmark the site, follow these steps:

1. Tap the Add icon at the bottom of the screen (refer to Figure 5.2).

   In the sheet that appears, the first option is Add Bookmark. (I look at the other options later in this chapter.)

2. Tap Add Bookmark.

   The Add Bookmark screen opens, displaying the name of the book-mark (**Figure 5.7**). If the name is too long for your liking, edit it with the standard keyboard.

Figure 5.7
*Creating a
bookmark.*

3. Tap the location entry (which in Figure 5.7 reads My Faves), and choose a location for your bookmark.

   When you do this, a list that contains your bookmarks-folder hierarchy appears. Tap the folder where you'd like to file your bookmark. From now on, this folder is where you'll find that bookmark.

4. Tap Save to save the bookmark in this location, or tap Cancel to end the bookmarking operation.

Organizing and editing bookmarks

If you're as organized as I am (meaning not very), your bookmarks may be a bit of a mess. Although you're better off organizing the bookmarks on your computer and then syncing them to your device, you can organize them on the iPhone or iPod touch as well. To do so, follow along:

1. Tap the Bookmarks icon.

2. In the resulting Bookmarks screen, tap the Edit button.

3. To delete an item, tap the red minus (–) icon that appears next to it.

The red minus icon appears next to all entries in the screen save Reading List, History, Bookmarks Bar, and Bookmarks Menu—in short, all the items you've created but none of the items that the device requires.

You'll also notice the three-line reposition icon to the right of these marked items, indicating that you can change the items' positions in the list by dragging the icons up or down. You can also rename your bookmark, change its URL, or file it in a different folder by tapping its name while in editing mode (which you enter after tapping the Edit button) and then making those changes in the resulting Edit Bookmark screen.

Additionally, you can create a new folder this way:

1. Tap the New Folder icon in the bottom-right corner of the screen to open an Edit Folder screen.

2. Use the onscreen keyboard to give your folder a name; then choose a location for it by tapping the field below the name entry.

   This field displays the name of the folder you're currently in (such as Bookmarks Bar).

3. Tap this field.

   Up pops the bookmarks hierarchy.

4. Tap the folder in which you'd like to place this new folder.

5. Tap the arrow icon in the top-left corner of the screen.

   Your folder is created.

Getting more from the Add icon

As I mention in "Creating bookmarks" earlier in this chapter, when you tap the Add icon at the bottom of Safari's screen, you see other options after Add Bookmark. Those options are Add to Reading List, Add to Home Screen, Mail Link to This Page, Tweet, Print, and Cancel. These buttons work this way:

- **Add to Reading List.** Reading List (see the sidebar about it earlier in this chapter) is a place for storing Web pages that you want to return to later. Tap this button to add items to your Reading List.

- **Add to Home Screen.** When you tap this button, an Add to Home screen appears, displaying the name of the Web page you're currently viewing, with some kind of icon next to the page's name (**Figure 5.8**). (Some Web sites have gone to the trouble of creating a cool icon that looks great on iOS devices; other icons are just undistinguished thumbnails of a portion of the page.) You're welcome to rename the saved page by using the keyboard.

Figure 5.8
Adding a Web site to your Home screen.

Tap the Add button, and an icon representing that Web page is created on the Home screen (**Figure 5.9**). In the future, when you tap that icon, Safari will launch and take you directly to that page.

Figure 5.9
A Web page's icon on the Home screen.

- **Mail Link to This Page.** If you find a Web page that cries out to be shared with your nearest as well as dearest, tap Mail Link to This Page. When you do, a new, unaddressed email message opens. The Subject heading is the name of the Web page, and the body of the message contains a link to the page. All you need to do is address the message and tap Send.

- **Tweet.** iOS adds a fair dollop of Twitter integration, and this sheet is one place where you find it. If you have a Twitter account and want to tweet a link to this site, tap the Tweet button. When you do, a Tweet window appears, along with the device's keyboard. Type some text, tap Add Location if you'd like to append your location to the tweet, and then tap Send. The resulting tweet contains the link along with your message. (You can add your Twitter user name and password by going back to the Home screen and tapping Settings > Twitter.)

- **Print.** If you have a printer that's compatible with your iPhone or iPod touch, you can use the Print command to print the contents of the Web page to it. (I discuss printing in Chapter 10.)

- **Cancel.** Tap this command to do just that.

Setting Safari

Like other iOS applications, Safari has its own collection of settings. As you might guess, you find them by tapping Settings > Safari (**Figure 5.11**).

Figure 5.11
Safari's settings screen.

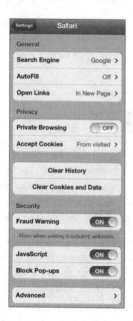

These settings include the following:

Search Engine. The iPhone and iPod touch can use Google, Yahoo, or Bing for its Web searches. Choose the one you want here.

AutoFill. AutoFill, like your computer's Web browser, can fill in contact information, user names, and passwords. To enable those options, tap AutoFill, and toggle the Use Contact Info and Names & Passwords sliders to On. By default, when you enable the Use Contact Info option, the device uses the information from the contact that contains your information. You can change the contact information that the iPhone or iPod touch uses by tapping the current My Info entry and choosing a different contact from the list that appears.

Open Links. You can choose to open links in a new page or open them in the background (creating another page that you access by tapping the Pages icon).

Private Browsing. When this option is on, the iPhone or iPod touch keeps no record of where you travel on the Internet.

Accept Cookies. Many Web sites leave little markers called *cookie*s in your Web browser. Cookies can store information such as when you visited the site and which pages you saw there. Sometimes, they also store information such as your user name and password for that site.

The Accept Cookies setting gives you a measure of control:

- You can choose never to accept cookies (which some people consider to be more secure and private, but which forces you to reenter passwords and user names each time you return).

- You can opt to accept just those cookies sent by each site you visit. (Some sites plant cookies from their advertisers, and this option prevents that behavior.)

- You can choose to always accept cookies, which means that your device is now a cookie-gathering machine.

The default setting is From Visited, which I think nicely balances privacy and convenience.

Clear History, Clear Cookies and Data. These two buttons in the Safari Settings screen allows you to wipe your tracks:

- Earlier, I told you that when you start typing a URL in Safari's Address field, the device makes suggestions based on past searches. To stop this behavior, tap Clear History.

- If you're concerned that the iPhone's or iPod touch's stored cookies may reveal more about your browsing habits than you're comfortable with, tap Clear Cookies and Data.

Cookies can also contain such information as your login data, which you'll have to reenter if you clear cookies and data.

When you tap either of these buttons, you're asked to confirm that you really want to perform the action.

Fraud Warning. Your iPhone or iPod touch warns you when it believes that you're about to enter a fraudulent Web site. Such a site may claim to belong to your bank or credit-card company, for example, but exists only to steal money from people who unwarily provide their account information.

JavaScript. JavaScript is a scripting language that helps make Web sites more interactive. By default, Safari allows JavaScript to work. If you care to disable JavaScript for some reason, you do it with this On/Off switch.

Block Pop-Ups. I make a lot of my living by writing for advertising-based Web sites, but I've yet to see a pop-up window that did more than annoy me. If you're haunted by pop-up ads, leave this option's switch set to On.

Advanced. Tap this button to see two additional entries on the Advanced screen: Website Data and Debug Console. Tap the first to learn how much data is stored by each Web site that you've visited. You can delete each site's stored data individually by tapping the Edit button and then the Delete button, or clear it all by tapping Remove All Website Data at the bottom of the screen.

You can turn on a debug console within Safari if you're interested in seeing any coding errors that a Web page may contain. If you're an über-geek and find such errors fascinating, knock yourself out; switch it on. Everyone else, feel free to leave it off.

The Media Player

6

Sure, your iPhone and iPod touch are handy devices for surfing the Web, grabbing your email, and discovering just how much you've lost in the stock market on a given day. But there's a good reason why the Music app occupies such a prominent place in the Dock. Multitalented though these devices may be, they're also great media players. This chapter focuses on the media capabilities of the iPhone and iPod touch, and shows you how to make the most of them.

Getting the Goods

"Eep!" I hear you squeep. "I've never used iTunes or owned an iOS device. I have no idea how to get music into iTunes, much less put it on my iPhone or iPod touch. What do I do?"

Relax. I'm not going to tell you how to put your music and movies on your device until you know how to assemble a music and movie library.

I'll start with music. You have three ways to get tunes into iTunes:

- Recording (or ripping, in today's terminology) an audio CD

- Importing music that doesn't come directly from a CD (such as an audio track you downloaded or created in an audio application on your computer)

- Purchasing music from an online emporium such as Apple's iTunes Store

The following sections tell you how to use the first two methods. The iTunes Store is a special-enough place that I give it a separate chapter (Chapter 7).

note
The procedures for adding movies and videos are similar except that iTunes offers no option for ripping DVDs. You can do that, but the procedure is more complicated than ripping an audio CD.

Rip a CD

Apple intended the process of converting audio-CD music to computer data to be painless, and it is. Here's how to go about it:

1. Launch iTunes.

2. Insert an audio CD into your computer's CD or DVD drive, if it has one.

note Apple's Mac mini and MacBook Air don't carry such drives. You can add an external media drive to these devices via one of the computer's ports.

By default, iTunes tries to identify the CD you inserted. It logs on to the Web to download the CD's track information—a very handy feature for those who find typing minutiae to be tedious.

The CD appears in iTunes' Source list below the Devices heading, and the track info appears in the Song list to the right (**Figure 6.1**).

Figure 6.1
A selected CD and its tracks.

Then iTunes displays a dialog box, asking whether you'd like to import the tracks from the CD into your iTunes Library.

3. Click Yes, and iTunes imports the songs; click No, and it doesn't.

note You can change this behavior in iTunes' Preferences window. In the General preferences tab, you find a When You Insert a CD pop-up menu. Make a choice from that menu to direct iTunes to show the CD, begin playing it, ask to import it (the default), import it without asking, or import and then eject it.

4. If you decided earlier to not import the audio but want to do so now, simply select the CD in the Source list and click the Import CD button in the bottom-right corner of the iTunes window.

iTunes begins encoding the files via the method set in the Import Settings dialog box (**Figure 6.2**), which you access by clicking the Import Settings button at the bottom of the iTunes window or by opening iTunes' Preferences dialog box (choose iTunes > Preferences on a Mac or Edit > Preferences on a Windows PC), clicking the General

tab, and clicking the Import Settings button. By default, iTunes
imports songs in iTunes Plus AAC format at 256 Kbps.

Figure 6.2
*iTunes' import
settings.*

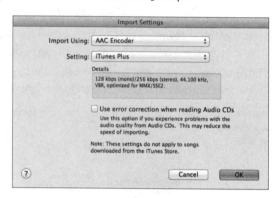

 To import only certain songs, clear the check boxes next to the titles of
songs you don't want to import; then click the Import CD button.

5. Click the Music entry in the Source list.

You'll find the songs you just imported somewhere in the list.

6. To listen to a song, click its name in the list and then click the Play
icon or press the spacebar.

Move music into iTunes

Ripping CDs isn't the only way to put music files on your computer.
Suppose that you've downloaded some audio files from the Web and
want to put them in iTunes. You have three ways to do that:

■ In iTunes, choose File > Add to Library.

When you choose this command, the Add To Library dialog box
appears (**Figure 6.3**). Navigate to the file, folder, or volume you want to

add to iTunes, and click Open. iTunes determines which files it thinks it can play and adds them to the library.

Figure 6.3
Navigate to the tracks you want to add to iTunes via the Add To Library dialog box.

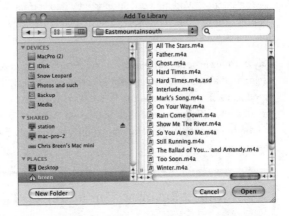

- Drag files, folders, or entire volumes to the iTunes icon in Mac OS X's Dock, the iTunes icon in Windows' Start menu (if you've pinned iTunes to this menu), or the iTunes icon in either operating system (at which point iTunes launches and adds the dragged files to its library).

- Drag files, folders, or entire volumes into iTunes' main window or the Library entry in the Source list.

  In the Mac versions of iTunes, by default you'll find songs in the iTunes Music folder within the iTunes folder inside the Music folder inside your Mac OS X user folder. The path to my iTunes music files, for example, would be chris/Music/iTunes/iTunes Music.

  Windows users will find their iTunes Music folder by following this path: *yourusername*/My Music (XP) or Music/iTunes/iTunes Music (Vista and Windows 7).

You can use the same methods to add compatible videos and movies to your iTunes Library. (For more on what makes those videos compatible, see the sidebar "Working with Supported Video Formats" later in the chapter.) Those videos will most likely appear in the Movies playlist in the Source list.

I say *most likely* because there are a few exceptions: Videos specifically designated as music videos appear in the Music playlist, videos designated as TV shows appear in the TV Shows playlist, and video podcasts are filed under Podcasts in iTunes' Source list. See the sidebar "Tag, You're It" later in this chapter for information on how to apply those video designations.

Import Business: Combining CD Tracks

There may be occasions when you don't want iTunes to extract individual tracks from a CD, such as when you have a long audiobook that's stored on multiple CDs, and each CD has a dozen or more individual files that represent portions of chapters. Managing what may turn out to be dozens of chapters on an iPhone or iPod touch is anything but convenient. To work around a problem like this one, you can combine all the tracks on the CD into a single long track.

To do that, insert the CD, turn down iTunes' offer to rip the CD for you, select the CD in iTunes' Source list, select all the tracks on the CD, and choose Advanced > Join CD Tracks. The contents of the CD will be ripped as one long file.

Creating and Configuring Playlists

Before you put any media files (music or video) on your iPhone or iPod touch, organize them in iTunes. Doing so will make it far easier to find the media you want, both on your computer and on your device. The best way to organize that material is through playlists.

A *playlist* is simply a set of tracks and/or videos that you believe should be grouped. The organizing principle is completely up to you. You can organize songs by artist, by mood, by style, by song length . . . heck, if you like, you can have iTunes automatically gather all your 1958 doo-wop tunes with the letter *z* in their titles. Similarly, you can organize your videos by criteria including director, actor, and TV-series title. You can mix videos and music tracks within playlists as well, combining, say, music videos and music tracks by the same artist. As far as playlists are concerned, you're the boss.

The following sections look at ways to create playlists.

tip   You can also create playlists directly on your device, as you see in the sidebar "Creating and Editing Playlists on the iPhone and iPod touch" later in this chapter.

Standard playlists

Standard playlists are those that you make by hand, selecting each of the media files you want to group. To create a standard playlist in iTunes, follow these steps:

1. Click the large plus (+) icon in the bottom-left corner of the iTunes window, or choose File > New Playlist (Command-N on the Mac, Ctrl+N in Windows).

2. In the highlighted field that appears next to your new playlist in the Source list, type a name for that playlist.

3. Click an appropriate entry in the Source list—Music, Movies, TV Shows, or Podcasts—and select the tracks or videos you want to place in the playlist you created.

4. Drag the selected tracks or videos to the new playlist's icon.

5. Arrange the order of the tracks or videos in your new playlist.

   To do this, click the Number column in the main window, and drag tracks up and down in the list. When the iPhone or iPod touch is synchronized with iTunes, this order is how the songs will appear in the playlist on your device.

   If the songs in your playlist come from the same album, and you want the songs in the playlist to appear in the same order as they do on the original album, click the Album heading.

Playlist from selection

You can also create a new playlist from selected items by following these steps:

1. Command-click (Mac) or Ctrl+click (Windows) songs or videos to select the files you'd like to appear in the new playlist.

2. Choose File > New Playlist from Selection (Command-Shift-N on a Mac, Ctrl+Shift+N on a Windows PC).

   A new playlist containing the selected items will appear below the Playlists heading in the iTunes Source list. If all selected tracks are from the same album, the list bears the name of the artist and album. If the tracks are from different albums by the same artist, the playlist is named after the artist. If you've mixed tracks by different artists

or combined music with videos, the new playlist displays the name
untitled playlist.

3. To name (or rename) the playlist, type in the highlighted field.

Smart Playlists

Smart Playlists are slightly different beasts. They include tracks that
meet certain conditions you've defined—for example, Neil Young tracks
encoded in AAC format that are shorter than 4 minutes.

Creating a Smart Playlist

Here's how to work the magic of a basic Smart Playlist:

1. In iTunes, choose File > New Smart Playlist (Command-Option-N on
the Mac, Ctrl+Alt+N in Windows).

You can also hold down the Option key on the Mac or the Shift key on
a Windows PC and then click the gear icon that replaces the plus icon
at the bottom of the iTunes window.

2. Choose your criteria in the Smart Playlist dialog box.

You'll spy a pop-up menu that allows you to select items by various
criteria—including artist, composer, genre, podcast, bit rate, comment,
date added, and last played—followed by a Contains field. To choose
all songs by Elvis Presley and Elvis Costello, for example, you'd choose
Artist from the pop-up menu and then enter **Elvis** in the Contains
field (**Figure 6.4**).

Figure 6.4
*The inner
workings of a
simple Smart
Playlist.*

You can limit the selections that appear in the playlist by minutes, hours, megabytes, gigabytes, or number of songs. You may want the playlist to contain no more than 2 GB worth of songs and videos, for example.

You'll also see a Live Updating option. When it's switched on, this option ensures that if you add to iTunes any songs or videos that meet the criteria you've set, those files will be added to the playlist. If you add a new Elvis Costello album to iTunes, for example, iTunes updates your Elvis Smart Playlist automatically.

3. Click OK.

A new playlist that contains your smart selections appears in iTunes' Source list.

You don't have to settle for a single criterion. By clicking the plus icon next to a criterion field, you can add other conditions. You could create a playlist containing, say, only songs you've never listened to by salsa artists whose names contain the letter *x*.

Genius playlists and Mixes

With iTunes 8, Apple introduced the compelling Genius feature. When you turn on Genius, you voluntarily (and anonymously) submit the contents of your iTunes Library to Apple. In exchange, Apple analyzes that content and sends a database file of related music in your library back to your computer. Using this file, Genius can create playlists of music that it believes will work well with a track that you've selected.

Say that you select The Rolling Stones' "19th Nervous Breakdown" as the source track in iTunes and then click the Genius icon at the bottom of the iTunes window. Genius creates a playlist of 25 tracks that includes classic rock tracks from your iTunes Library—Donovan's "Mellow Yellow," The Allman Brothers' "Whipping Post," and Deep Purple's "Hush," for example.

In addition to Genius playlists, iTunes 10 can create *Genius Mixes,* which are 250-track playlists chosen by genre from your iTunes Library. In the following sections, I look at the ins and outs of each feature.

Tag, You're It

So how does iTunes know about tracks, artists, albums, and genres? Through something called ID3 tags. *ID3 tags* are just little bits of data included in a song file that tell programs like iTunes something about the file—not just the track's name and the album it came from, but also the composer, the album track number, the year it was recorded, and whether it's part of a compilation.

These ID3 tags are the keys to creating great Smart Playlists. To view this information, select a track and choose File > Get Info. Click the Info tab of the resulting dialog box, and you'll see fields for all kinds of things. You may find occasions when it's helpful to change the information in these fields. If you have two versions of the same song—perhaps one is a studio recording and another is a live recording—you could change the title of the latter to include *(Live).*

A really useful field to edit is Comments. Here, you can enter anything you like and then use that entry to sort your music. If a particular track would be great to fall asleep to, for example, enter **sleepy** in the Comments field. Do likewise with similar tracks, and when you're ready to hit the hay, create a Smart Playlist that includes *Comment is sleepy.* With this technique under your belt, you can create playlists that fit particular moods or situations, such as a playlist that gets you pumped up during a workout.

Genius playlists

To create Genius playlists with iTunes, follow these steps:

1. Switch on the Genius feature.

   When you install iTunes, you're offered the choice to turn Genius on. Doing so requires an iTunes account. If you don't have one, no worries; when you start the Genius process, you'll find an option for signing up for an account. If you neglected to turn on Genius, you can do so by choosing Store > Turn on Genius. If you're connected to the Internet, iTunes will ask you to sign in to your iTunes account.

2. Wait while iTunes configures Genius.

   iTunes gathers information about your music library—specifically, the songs it contains—and sends that information to Apple's servers anonymously. That information is compared with similar data from other users and placed in a database. A database file that contains the relationship data is sent back to your computer.

3. Create a Genius playlist.

   Select a track in your iTunes Library, and click the Genius button in the bottom-right corner of the iTunes window. iTunes will create a new playlist of 25 songs (by default) that should go well with the track you selected. You can ask Genius to create a longer version of this playlist by making a larger choice from the Limit To pop-up menu at the top of the window; your choices are 25, 50, 75, and 100 songs. You can also click Refresh to ask Genius to try again.

4. Save the playlist.

   When you click the Save Playlist button (also at the top of the window), iTunes creates a playlist named after your source track— *A Common Disaster*, for example. You can return to any Genius playlist you've created and change the Limit To settings as well as refresh the playlist.

5. Expose the Genius sidebar.

Click the Sidebar icon in the bottom-right corner of the iTunes window to display the Genius sidebar, which is designed to recommend related music from the iTunes Store (**Figure 6.5**).

At the top of the sidebar, you'll find entries that include the name of the artist, Also by This Artist (which includes Top Albums and Top Songs entries), and Genius Recommendations. You might also see an iTunes Essentials entry. A small arrow icon next to an entry indicates a potential trip to the iTunes Store. Click an artist's name, for example, and you'll be taken to the store page devoted to that artist. Click the arrow icon next to Genius Recommendations, and iTunes creates a list of those recommendations. (Though this list looks like a playlist, you can't save it as such.)

Figure 6.5
The Genius sidebar.

Next to the song selections, you'll see both a Preview button (denoted by a small Play icon) and a Buy button. To audition 30 seconds of a track, just click the Preview button. If you like what you've heard and would like to own the track, click Buy. In the resulting dialog box, you'll be prompted for your Apple ID and password. Enter that info and click the Buy button, and the track downloads to your computer.

note   You can sync Genius playlists to your iPhone or iPod touch just as you can any other playlists.

Genius Mixes

Genius Mixes were introduced in iTunes 9 and, as I write this chapter, are supported only by 2G and later iPod touches, the 5G and 6G iPod nano, the iPhone, and the iPad. Genius Mixes are broader tools than Genius playlists in that they're created based on genres—Rock, Jazz, and Classical, for example.

The "genius" of Genius Mixes is that their content is still related, much like the content of Genius playlists. Unless you have a small music library, it's unlikely that iTunes will produce a Genius Mix including AC/DC, Donovan, Sheryl Crow, and Ry Cooder, even though all four artists may have had a Rock genre tag applied to them. Instead, you may have one Classic Mix that includes '60s artists such as Janis Joplin, Cream, Jimi Hendrix, and The Small Faces. Another Mainstream Rock Mix could include Bruce Springsteen, Huey Lewis & The News, Tom Petty and the Heartbreakers, and Eric Clapton. So thanks to the enormous database of related music first created when the Genius feature was introduced with iTunes 8, iTunes has the power to create these large mixes that make sense.

Creating them is really easy:

1. Launch iTunes.

2. Click the Genius Mixes entry, located below the Genius heading in iTunes' Source list.

   If you don't see the Genius Mixes entry, hover your cursor over Genius in the Source list, and click the word *Show* to the right. The Genius and Genius Mixes entries appear.

iTunes will create up to 12 Genius Mixes. Each Genius Mix is represented by an album cover that, in turn, features four album covers taken from the music in that Genius Mix (**Figure 6.6**). An example Contemporary Folk

Mix could contain artwork from albums by The Weepies, Patty Griffin, Neil Young, and Rosie Thomas.

Figure 6.6
Genius Mixes.

Unlike Genius playlists, Genius Mixes can't be edited. In fact, you can't even see the contents of one of these mixes. What iTunes provides is exactly what you get. To play one, just click its icon, and the first track in the mix plays. To skip to the next track, click the Next button in iTunes' play controls (located in the top-left corner of the iTunes window) or press your keyboard's right-arrow key.

To sync Genius Mixes, do this:

1. Select your device in iTunes' Source list.

2. Click the Music tab.

3. Enable the Sync Music option.

4. Enable the Selected Playlists, Artists, and Genres option.

5. In the Playlists column, look for the Genius Mixes entry; then select all of these mixes (by checking the Genius Mixes check box) or specific mixes (**Figure 6.7**).

Figure 6.7
Selecting Genius Mixes.

Playlists
- ☐ Purchased
- ▼ ☐ Genius Mixes
  - ☐ Classic R&B Mix
  - ☐ Folk Rock Mix
  - ☑ Folk Rock Mix
  - ☐ Adult Alternative Rock Mix
  - ☐ Mainstream Rock Mix
  - ☐ Jazz Mix
  - ☐ Indie Rock & Lo-Fi Mix
  - ☐ Alternative Pop/Rock Mix
  - ☑ Adult Alternative Pop Mix
  - ☐ British Invasion Mix
  - ☑ Punk Mix
  - ☐ Americana Mix

6. Sync the iPhone or iPod touch.

When you sync a Genius Mix to your device, a new Genius icon appears at the bottom of the Music app's screen. Tap Genius, and you can select the Genius Mixes on the device and play them simply by tapping the Play icon in the center of the screen.

tip If you choose to sync all your music with the iPhone or iPod touch, Genius Mixes are included automatically. If you don't have enough room on the device to sync your entire music library, however, Genius Mixes won't be added—which makes sense, as each Genius Mix can include up to 250 tracks.

Using the Music App

Now that you've filled your device with tunes, you'd probably like to know how to find and play them. Follow along as I walk through the Music app.

Cover Flow view

Tap the orange Music icon in the Dock of your iPhone's or iPod touch's Home screen, wait for the Playlists screen to appear (which it does by default when you first tap Music), and immediately turn the device on its side. You're witnessing Cover Flow view, which lets you browse your music collection by its album or program artwork (**Figure 6.8**). I don't care if you never choose to browse your music this way; Cover Flow is the music feature you'll choose first to impress your friends. They can't help but *oooh* in awe when you flick your finger across the screen and the artwork flips by.

Figure 6.8
Cover Flow view on the iPhone and iPod touch.

David Bowie
Hunky-Dorey

Should you want to navigate your music in Cover Flow view, you can do so easily:

1. Turn the device to landscape orientation (it doesn't matter whether this turn places the Home button on the right or left side; the button works either way), and flick your finger across the display to move through your audio collection.

Albums are sorted by the artist's first name, so *Al Green* appears near the beginning and *ZZ Top* appears close to the end.

2. When you find an album you want to listen to, tap its cover.

The artwork flips around and reveals the track list of the album's contents (**Figure 6.9**).

Figure 6.9
An iPhone or iPod touch track list.

As with other lists that may be longer than the device's screen, you're welcome to flick your finger up the display to move down through the list.

3. Tap the track you want to listen to.

Playback begins from that track and plays to the end of the list in the order presented in the track list.

To adjust volume in this view, use the volume controls on the side of the device. To pause playback, tap the Play/Pause icon in the bottom-left corner of the screen or (if you're listening with the optional headset that includes controls) press the headset's Center button once.

4. To move to another album, tap the album-art thumbnail in the top-right corner of the cover, swipe your finger to the right or left, or tap the *i* icon in the bottom-right corner of the screen.

Any of these actions flips the track list back to the artwork.

note While you're listening to the contents of one album, you're free to view the contents of another. Just flick your finger across the screen to move through your collection. Go ahead and tap an album to see its contents. It won't play until you tap a track.

Music Now Playing screen

Turn your device so that it's in portrait orientation, and Cover Flow disappears; it works only in landscape orientation. What you're left with when you flip the iPhone or iPod touch to portrait orientation is the Music Now Playing screen. You use this screen to perform several tasks, including navigating through an album, fast-forwarding, switching on shuffle or repeat play, and rating your tracks. This screen differs from the Now Playing screen that you see when playing a video, podcast, or audiobook. (I discuss how it differs later in the chapter.)

This Now Playing screen has two main views: standard play and track list.

Standard play

The view you see first is straightforward. From the bottom of the screen to the top, you see a volume slider; play controls that include Previous/Rewind, Play/Pause, and Next/Fast Forward icons; AirPlay; album art; a Back icon; artist, track title, and album title information; and a Track List icon (**Figure 6.10**).

Figure 6.10
The Music Now Playing screen.

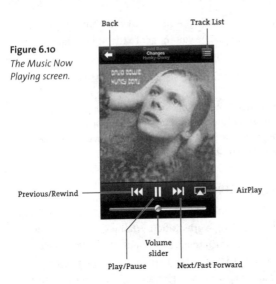

Back

Track List

Previous/Rewind

AirPlay

Volume slider

Play/Pause

Next/Fast Forward

note You won't see an AirPlay icon if your device isn't on the same local network as AirPlay–compatible devices such as Apple's AirPort Express Base Station or Apple TV. Similarly, if you don't have any AirPlay devices, the AirPlay icon won't appear.

The volume slider operates like its real-world equivalent. Just drag the silver ball on the slider to the right to increase volume and to the left to turn the volume down. (You can also use the device's mechanical volume buttons or the volume controls on a compatible set of headphones.)

The Previous/Rewind icon earns its double name because of its two jobs. Tap it once, and you're taken to the beginning of the currently play-ing track or chapter of the currently playing podcast or audiobook. Tap it twice, and you move to the previous track or chapter. Tap and hold, and the currently playing track rewinds.

The Play/Pause icon toggles between these two functions.

The Next/Fast Forward icon works like Previous/Rewind: Tap once to move to the next track in the track list or chapter in an audiobook or podcast; press and hold to fast-forward through the currently playing track.

I'll skip album art for a second and move to the Back icon in the top-left corner of the screen. Tap this icon, and you move to the currently selected track-view screen. If you've chosen to view your music by playlist, for example, you'll see your list of playlists. When you tap the Back icon and are taken to one of these screens, a Now Playing icon appears in the top-right corner of the current screen. This icon appears whenever you're in the Music app, making it easy to move to the Now Playing screen.

Track list

In the top-right corner of the Music Now Playing screen is the Track List icon. Tap this icon, and you get that album-cover flip effect again and a list of the current album's contents (**Figure 6.11**). (Naturally, if you have only a couple of tracks from that album on your device, you see just those tracks.) Just as you can in Cover Flow view, tap an entry in the track list to listen to that track. Again, tracks play in order from where you tapped.

Figure 6.11
A track list in the Music Now Playing screen.

The Track List screen also includes a means for rating tracks. Just above the track list, you'll see five gray dots. To assign a star rating from 1 to 5, simply tap one of the dots. Tap the fourth dot, for example, and the first four dots turn to stars. You can also wipe your finger across the dots to add or remove stars. These ratings are transferred to iTunes when you next sync your device. Tap the album-artwork image to flip the track list and return to the Now Playing screen.

Additional controls

While you're in the Music Now Playing screen, tap the artwork in the middle of the screen, and additional controls drop down from above (**Figure 6.12**).

Figure 6.12
Tap the Music Now Playing screen to see additional controls.

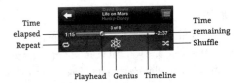

Time elapsed — Repeat — Time remaining — Shuffle

Playhead Genius Timeline

In the center of these controls is a timeline with playhead. To the left of the timeline is the location of the playhead in minutes and seconds—1:40, for example. To the right of the timeline is the track's remaining time. Drag the playhead with your finger to move to a different position in the currently playing track. You can do this while a track is playing nd hear where you are as your drag (or *scrub*, as it's known in the iTunes business).

Below the timeline, on the left side of the screen, you'll find a Repeat icon. Tap this icon once, and the contents of the currently playing album, audiobook, or podcast repeat from beginning to end. Tap the Repeat icon twice, and just the currently playing selection repeats.

Next to the Repeat icon is the Genius icon. As you saw earlier in this chapter, Genius is a very cool feature—so cool, in fact, that it deserves to be called out separately (and I do that in the next section).

To the right of Genius is the Shuffle icon. Tap this icon once so that it turns blue and the contents of the current album are shuffled; tap it again to turn shuffle off.

note If you've added lyrics to a track (as you can in the Lyrics tab of the track's Info window in iTunes), those lyrics also appear on the device's screen when you enter this view. If you'd rather not display lyrics or podcast information on your iPhone or iPod touch running iOS 4, tap Settings > Music, and flip the Lyrics & Podcasts Info switch to Off.

More-Refined Scrubbing

If you used the iPhone's or iPod touch's scrubbing feature before the 3.0 software, you know how difficult it was to locate the exact spot you wanted in a track; scrubbing wasn't a precision operation. That changed with the iOS 3 software. Now you can scrub in smaller increments than ever before.

To do that, tap and hold the playhead. When you do (and if your thumb doesn't get in the way), you'll see the words *Hi-Speed Scrubbing*. If you drag your finger to the left or right, you move through the track in large increments. Ah, but drag your finger *down* the screen, and those words change to *Half Speed Scrubbing, Quarter Speed Scrubbing,* and *Fine Scrubbing.* Keep dragging until you find an increment you're happy with and then drag your finger to the left or right. The farther down the display your finger is, the smaller the increments the playhead jumps in.

True Genius

After you've enabled the Genius feature in iTunes and synced your device, you can create Genius playlists on your iPhone or iPod touch. Here's the first of two ways to do this:

1. Launch the Music app, and tap Playlists at the bottom of the resulting screen.

2. Tap Genius Playlist at the top of the screen.

   The Songs screen appears.

3. Tap a song that you want to use as the basis of the Genius playlist.

   The device constructs a playlist of up to 25 tracks (including the one you selected) that it believes are related, and the track you selected starts playing.

4. Tap the Back icon to view the playlist.

   Doing so takes you to the Genius Playlist screen, where you see the list of tracks (**Figure 6.13**). To create a new Genius playlist, tap New, and the process begins again. To have the iPhone or iPod touch construct a different playlist based on the same selection, tap Refresh. Finally, if you want to save your playlist, tap Save.

Figure 6.13
*The Genius
Playlist screen.*

When you tap Save, Genius creates a playlist that bears the name of the selected track. So, for example, if you based a Genius playlist on "Here Comes the Sun," the playlist will be called *Here Comes the Sun*. Its name is followed by a Genius icon in the list of playlists so that you know its origin.

Or...

1. While viewing the Music Now Playing screen, tap the screen so that the timeline appears near the top of the screen; then tap the Genius icon below the timeline (refer to Figure 6.12 earlier in this chapter).

   The progress icon appears briefly, followed by a Genius screen that features, at the top, the song you selected as the basis for the playlist. The up-to-24 additional songs appear below it.

2. Create a new Genius playlist, try again, or save the playlist.

   When you sync your device to your Mac or PC, the Genius playlists you created on your iPhone or iPod touch appear in your computer's copy of iTunes, marked with the Genius icon.

Music content views

The iPhone's and iPod touch's Music app provides several ways to organize your media. Look across the bottom of the screen (anywhere but in the Now Playing screen), and you'll see five icons for doing just that: Playlists; Artists; Songs; Albums; and More, which leads you to even more options.

note If you've synced a Genius Mix to your device, those icons will be Genius, Playlists, Artists, Songs, and More (*Figure 6.14*).

Figure 6.14
Icons at the bottom of a Music-app screen.

These icons are largely self-explanatory. If you've synced a Genius Mix to your device, it (and others you've synced) are playable when you tap Genius. To play one, just tap the Play icon on the screen. To navigate to other Genius Mixes, swipe your finger from right to left.

When you tap Playlists, you'll see a list of all the playlists you've synced to your device. Tap a playlist to move to a screen where all the tracks on the playlist appear in the order in which they were arranged in iTunes. If you tapped the Album heading when the playlist was displayed in iTunes, for example, the tracks appear in that order. Tap a track, and you're taken to the Now Playing screen, where the track begins playing.

Whenever you choose a list of tracks in one of these views, Shuffle is the obvious entry at the top of the list. (I say *obvious* because if you flick down, the Search field appears, thus becoming the first entry.) Tap Shuffle, and the contents of that collection of tracks play in random order.

Tap Artists, and you're presented with an alphabetical list of the artists represented on your iPhone or iPod touch. If your device has tracks from more than one album by the selected artist, when you tap the artist's name, you'll be taken to that artist's screen, which displays the titles of the artist's represented albums (along with thumbnails of the cover art). To view tracks from a particular album, tap its name. To view all songs by the artist, tap All Songs in this screen.

The Songs screen lists all the songs on your iPhone or iPod touch. Like any list that contains several dozen (or more) entries, this one displays a tiny alphabet along the right side of the screen. To navigate to a letter quickly, tap it (as best you can, as the letters are really small) or slide your finger along the alphabet listing to dash through the list.

note If the first word of a list entry is *A* or *The*, the second word in the entry is used for sorting purposes. *The Beatles* is filed under *B*, for example, and *A Case of You* appears under *C*.

The Albums screen lists albums in alphabetical order and displays a thumbnail of the cover art next to the name of each album.

The iPhone's and iPod touch's displays have limited space, yet you have many more ways to organize your media—by audiobooks, compilations, composers, and genres, for example. That's exactly what the More icon is for. Tap it, and you'll see just those items I list, as well as iTunes U and Podcasts entries. Tap these entries, and most of them behave pretty much as you'd expect, with a couple of variations:

- The Compilations entry lists only those albums that iTunes denotes as compilations. These items are usually greatest-hits collections, soundtracks, or albums on which lots of artists appear, such as tribute albums or concert recordings.

- The Podcasts screen displays all the podcasts on your device, along with their cover art. Tap a podcast title, and you're taken to a screen that lists all that podcast's episodes. Blue dots denote podcasts that you haven't listened to yet.

More Mucking

Unhappy that Apple chose to tuck the Podcasts entry in the More screen, yet left Artists easily accessible at all times? No worries. You can change what appears at the bottom of the Music application. Simply tap More and then the Edit icon in the top-left corner of the screen. Doing so produces a Configure screen that swipes up from the bottom of the display. Here, you'll see all the music category entries listed. Find one you like, and drag it over a icon on the bottom of the screen that you want to replace. The new entry takes the place of the old one, and the old entry is listed in the More screen. When you're done, tap Done.

Applying Music App Settings

Like other iOS apps, the Music app get its own little entry in the iPhone's and iPod touch's Settings screen.

iTunes Match

By now, you're aware that through iTunes in the Cloud, you can download any music you've purchased from the iTunes Store. You may be unaware that for $25 a year, you can download not only this music, but also up to 25,000 tracks in your iTunes Library that you haven't purchased from Apple.

This process surely sounds like it would take days of uploading for a large music library, but it needn't be. When you initiate iTunes Match by choosing Turn on iTunes Match from iTunes' Store menu, iTunes creates a catalog of the music in your iTunes Library. It sends this catalog—not the music itself—to Apple. Any tracks in your music library that are also in Apple's catalog are made available to you for download. If your iTunes Library contains tracks that Apple doesn't have, it uploads them.

note Any tracks in your iTunes Library that you added via iTunes Match will be downloaded to you at a format of 256 Kbps AAC. This is a great thing if the original tracks were at a lower resolution—say, 128 Kbps MP3. Note, however, that any tracks you upload that aren't available from the iTunes Store remain in their original formats. If you uploaded a 128 Kbps MP3 file, for example, that's exactly what you'll be able to download.

Show All Music

When this option is switched on, your iPhone or iPod touch displays all the music it has access to—the music stored on your device, as well as any music available to you via iTunes in the Cloud and iTunes Match. Turn this option off, and you'll see just the music stored on your device.

Shake to Shuffle

If you'd like to engage the device's shuffle feature, just switch on this option and give your iPhone or iPod touch a vigorous shake. This shake does more than shuffle; it also immediately causes the device to stop playing the current song and move to another one. So even though you can't vent your frustration at a particularly awful song via Voice Control or Siri, you're free to shake the device violently while shouting "*I . . . hate . . . this . . . song!*"

Sound Check

iTunes includes a Sound Check feature that you can use to make the volumes of all your tracks similar. Without Sound Check, you may be listening to a Chopin prelude at a lovely, lilting volume and be scared out of your socks when the next track, AC/DC's "Highway to Hell," blasts through your brain. When Sound Check is on, each track should be closer to the same relative volume. For Sound Check to work on the iPhone or iPod touch, it must be enabled in iTunes' Playback preference. When it is, you can use it on your device by enabling it in this setting.

EQ

EQ (or *equalization*) is the process of boosting or cutting certain frequencies in the audio spectrum—making the low frequencies louder and the high frequencies quieter, for example. If you've ever adjusted the bass and treble controls on your home or car stereo, you get the idea.

The iPhone and iPod touch come with the same EQ settings as iTunes:

Off	Flat	R & B
Acoustic	Hip Hop	Rock
Bass Booster	Jazz	Small Speakers
Bass Reducer	Latin	Spoken Word
Classical	Loudness	Treble Booster
Dance	Lounge	Treble Reducer
Deep	Piano	Vocal Booster
Electronic	Pop	

Although you can listen to each EQ setting to get an idea of what it does, you may find it easier to open iTunes; choose Window > Equalizer; and then, in the resulting Equalizer window, choose the various EQ settings from the window's pop-up menu. The equalizer's ten band sliders will show you which frequencies have been boosted and which have been cut. Any slider that appears above the 0 dB line indicates a frequency that has been boosted. Conversely, sliders that appear below 0 dB indicate frequencies that have been cut.

Volume Limit

Though Apple takes pains to warn you in the iPhone and iPod touch documentation that blasting music into your ears at full volume can lead to hearing loss, some people just can't get enough volume. If your child is one of those people, consider setting a volume limit for the device's Headphone port. To do so, tap Volume Limit in the Music settings screen, and in the resulting Volume Limit screen, use the volume slider to set an acceptable volume. (Have a track playing when you do this so that you can listen to the effect.)

To keep your kid from changing your settings, tap Lock Volume Limit. You'll see a Set Code screen, where you'll enter and confirm a four-digit security code. When this code is set, the Lock Volume Limit icon changes to Unlock Volume Limit. Tap this button, and you'll be prompted for the security code.

Lyrics & Podcast Info

Earlier in the chapter, I mention that the iPhone and iPod touch have the ability to display lyrics and podcast information. You can display this text by tapping the Now Playing screen. (Lyrics first have to be added in iTunes. Podcast information is already embedded in podcasts that you obtain from the iTunes Store.) With this setting, you have the ability to turn lyrics and podcast information on or off.

Group by Album Artist

The tracks on some albums that feature multiple artists (think Willie Nelson and the many duets he's performed) won't be grouped as part of an album. If you turn this option on, these tracks should appear as a single album filed under the artist's name.

Home Sharing

Apple's Home Sharing technology allows you to stream music from your iTunes Library to any iOS device that has the same Apple ID and is on the same local network. To make it work, follow these steps.

1. Launch iTunes, and choose Advanced > Turn On Home Sharing *username*.

2. On your iPhone or iPod touch, tap Settings > Music.

3. In the Home Sharing area, enter your Apple ID and password.

4. Launch the Music app.

5. Tap More > Shared.

6. In the resulting screen, tap the name of your iTunes Library.

   Your device eventually loads the names of all the music in the iTunes Library on your computer.

7. Tap anything you'd like to play, just as you would tracks stored on your device.

   They stream across the network and play.

> **note** **This technique works with the Videos app too. Just launch Videos, and tap the Shared entry. Any movies, TV shows, music videos, and video podcasts in your iTunes Library will be available for streaming to your device.**

Using the Videos App

Like all iOS devices, the iPhone and iPod touch play videos. Despite a display that some people might consider to be small compared with the screen of an iPad or laptop, the iPhone and iPod touch screens are bright and plenty big enough for personal viewing. Here are the ins and outs of watching video on these devices.

Choosing and playing videos

To watch videos, naturally enough, you must launch the Videos app. By default, you'll find it in the Home screen. Playing videos in this app is straightforward. When you launch the app, the resulting screen lists

your videos in categories: Rented Movies (if any have been copied to the
device), Movies, TV Shows, Music Videos, and Podcasts (**Figure 6.15**).

Figure 6.15
Videos screen.

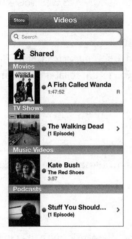

Each video has a thumbnail image of its artwork next to it. Depending
on the original source of the video, you may see title, artist, season, and
episode information. The Rented Movies section, for example, tells you
how many days you have left in the rental period to begin watching
each movie (or how many hours you have left to finish watching a movie
you've started). You'll definitely see the length of single videos—*1:56:26*,
for example. If you have multiple episodes of a TV show, you'll see the
name of the show as well as the number of episodes on the device.

To play a video, tap its list entry. Videos play only in landscape orientation,
regardless of which way you have the iPhone or iPod touch turned (yes,
even if you have portrait orientation lock switched on).

Applying Videos app settings

Yes, the Videos app has a settings screen as well. This is what it includes.

Start Playing

The first preference in the Video settings screen, Start Playing, lets you choose whether videos that you return to later play from where they left off or from the beginning.

Closed Captioning

Some videos that you purchase from the iTunes Store include closed captions. You can choose to show those captions by flicking this switch to On.

Home Sharing

As I discuss when talking about the Music app earlier in this chapter, the Video app also supports Home Sharing. Its implementation is just as slick for video.

The Stores

7

You know that constant use gives you the power to drain your iPhone's or iPod touch's battery. In what some people might view as a turnabout-is-fair-play situation, these devices have the power to drain your wallet. Their means for doing so are three Apple-owned online emporiums accessible from your device: the iTunes Store, the App Store, and the iBookstore.

The first store lets you browse, purchase, and download music, videos, podcasts, and iTunes U content over a Wi-Fi or 3G (iPhone only) connection with nothing more than your iPhone or iPod touch and an iTunes account linked to your credit card. (If you haven't yet created an iTunes account, page back to Chapter 2, where I discuss setting up your device.)

The App Store is where you find free and commercial add-on apps (made by Apple as well as third parties) that you can also download over Wi-Fi or 3G.

Finally, the iBookstore—available through the optional but free iBooks app—is your source for free as well as not-so-free e-books.

In this chapter, I examine the workings of all three stores.

The iTunes Store

You can download the same content offered by the iTunes Store directly to the iPhone or iPod touch. You can choose among the same millions of tracks, podcasts, TV shows, music videos, movies, and iTunes U content in this pocket-size version of the iTunes Store *and* in the iTunes Store available via iTunes. The feature works this way.

note To save wear and tear on your data plan, downloads over 3G are limited to 20 MB. Also, when you purchase or rent a high-definition (HD) movie or TV show with a iPhone or iPod touch, the HD version is downloaded to the device. When you purchase an HD movie or TV show, the standard-definition (SD) version will be made available for you to download to your computer. You don't get an SD version when you rent an HD video.

Tap the iTunes icon on the Home screen while you're connected to a Wi-Fi or 3G network, and the iTunes Store screen appears. Across the bottom of the screen, you see Music, Videos, Search, Purchased, and More icons. Tap More, and you see Genius, Ping, Tones, Podcasts, Audiobooks, iTunes U, and Downloads options. Here's what to expect.

Music

Tap Music, and you're taken to the store's Music section. Across the top of the screen are three buttons: New Releases, Top Tens, and Genres. These buttons work much as they do in the same-named areas of the full-grown iTunes Store's home page (which I hope you'll take the time to explore). Tap them to go to screens with the same names.

New Releases

Here, you see a list of the week's coolest additions—singles as well as albums. To preview or purchase one of these items, tap it to move to that item's screen. (I discuss the workings of this screen shortly.) In addition to the week's new releases, you're likely to see buttons for accessing free tracks and music videos and for viewing the hottest items currently available.

Near the bottom of the list of new releases, you'll see Complete My Album and Redeem items. Complete My Album is a feature you may use if you've purchased a track from an album and decide that you want to buy the rest of the album without paying twice for the track you already have. So tap this entry and then tap the album you want, and you'll find that you can purchase the rest of it for $9 rather than $9.99.

If you have an iTunes gift card or gift certificate, tap Redeem. In the resulting screen, tap the Code field, and the keyboard appears. After you enter the code, tap the Redeem button in the top-right corner of the screen to send the code to Apple.

At the very bottom of the New Releases screen is an Account button that displays the email address associated with your Apple ID—*example6@ mac.com*, for example—along with the amount of any credit you have (*$25 Credit*, perhaps, if you've redeemed an iTunes gift card). Tap that button, and you're offered the option to view your account details, sign out, tap an iForgot button that helps you reset a forgotten password, or tap Cancel to return to the Music screen.

Top Tens

This section features top songs and albums organized within particular genres. Tap Alternative, for example, and the next screen provides two large buttons: Top Songs and Top Albums (**Figure 7.1**). Tap one to see the top ten items of that kind. To see the complete list of Top Ten genres, tap the Ten More Songs button near the bottom of the screen.

Figure 7.1
A Top Tens screen.

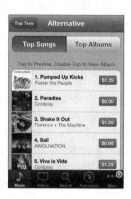

Genres

This section lists popular genres. What you see when you tap a genre depends on the genre. When I tap Rock, for example, I see New Releases; when I tap Hip Hop/Rap, I see titles offered below a Hot Albums, Singles, and EPs heading. Tapping Classical, Singer/Songwriter, or Jazz displays a list of albums. The top of each screen includes a couple of buttons that you can tap to go to albums that the store believes worthy of your attention.

Videos

The Videos area of the store is where you can rent or purchase movies, purchase TV shows or entire TV seasons, and buy music videos. Tap the Videos button at the bottom of the screen, and you see a layout similar to the Music screen, with three buttons across the top: Movies, TV Shows, and Music Videos.

The Music Info Screen

When you tap an album or track, you're taken to the information screen for that hunk of music. There, you'll find the artist's name, the album title, the album price (which you tap to purchase the item), Like, Post, X Person Who Owns This buttons (related to the Ping service, which I discuss later in this chapter), a reviews link that takes you to a screen of star-rated and commented reviews, and a list of album tracks that includes the price of each track. To preview a track, just tap it. When you tap a track, Like and Post buttons appear below the track (again, for Ping).

At the bottom of the screen, you may see More by This Artist, Profile, and Concerts links. (Popular artists have these links, whereas more obscure artists don't.) More by This Artist takes you to the artist's screen, where you can view top songs and albums by that artist. The Profile link takes you to the artist's Ping page, where you can choose to view more music by this artist as well as follow him, her, or them on Ping. Finally, Concerts shows you where the artist is playing, both around the world and locally. In the Concerts screen, you can indicate that you're going to the show and tap a Tickets button, whereupon Safari launches and takes you to the Ticketmaster Web site, where you can purchase tickets.

Movies

The Movies screen displays a couple of featured movies at the top (hot new releases and a link to 99-cent movie rentals, as I write this chapter). Below is a New Releases area; below that are Top Tens and Genres entries. Each entry lists the movie's genre (such as Comedy or Drama), its title, its user rating (1 to 5 stars, including half-stars), and the number of ratings it has received (*128 Ratings*, for example).

Tap a movie, and you see that movie's screen, where you can buy or rent it (if rental is an option—not all movies are for rent), as well as watch a preview of the movie. To do one of these things, tap the appropriate button.

Below the Buy and Rent buttons is a Reviews entry that displays a five-star scale, reflecting the average rating given by people who chose to submit reviews. These people may or may not have purchased or rented that movie from iTunes (and may not have seen it at all, so take some reviews with a grain of salt). Tap that entry, and you'll see the average rating and the number of people who have rated the movie. Below are user reviews, complete with title, text, date, and rating.

If you'd like to write a review of your own, tap the Write a Review button at the top of the Reviews screen. You'll be prompted for your iTunes password. Enter it, and you go to the Submit Review screen, where you can enter a rating, title, and review. To submit the review, just tap Send.

Below the Reviews entry for some movies, you'll find a Rotten Tomatoes rating. (Rotten Tomatoes is a popular Web site that aggregates critics' movie reviews.) These ratings provide a positive percentage rating (*62% positive*, for example) as well as a Rotten (green) or Fresh (red) tomato icon, indicating generally how good the movie is. Tap the rating, and you see a Rotten Tomatoes screen that features the Tomatometer (a gauge that measures fresh-to-rotten reviews); excerpts from some reviews; and a Read More on Rotten Tomatoes button that, when tapped, launches Safari and takes you to the Rotten Tomatoes site, where you can read even more reviews of the movie.

TV Shows

This section works almost exactly the same way as the Movies area. The main difference is that the items in this window are entire series (*The Walking Dead, Season 2,* for example) rather than single episodes. Tap a show, and you're taken to the season screen, where you can purchase individual episodes and sometimes entire seasons. These screens carry no Preview button. Instead, just tap an episode title, and the movie-player window displays a preview. If you'd like to find out more about an episode (and have the option to rent or purchase it), double-tap the entry. TV Shows screens also have a Reviews button.

Music Videos

Same idea here. You see a couple of featured items at the top of the screen, a list of music videos below, and Top Tens and Genres menus. Tap a video, and you see the Buy and Preview buttons, along with the tapworthy Reviews entry. In most cases, you also find a More by This Artist button. Tap it to see a screen listing other music videos by that artist.

Search

Tap this button, and a Search field appears. Tap this field, and the keyboard appears. Type a search term in the Search field; as you type, suggestions appear below. When the result you desire appears, tap it.

Purchased

As I mention in discussing iTunes in the Cloud (Chapter 2), now you can re-download any music or TV shows that you've purchased from the iTunes Store. Tap the Music button at the top of the screen, and you'll see All and Not on This iPhone/iPod buttons at the top. What they do is obvious. Below is a Recent Purchases entry that links to the most recent 250 purchases you've made. When you tap this button, you see your most recent purchases. You have the option to download individual items or (by tapping the Download All button in the top-right corner of the screen) all the tracks listed on this screen.

Below the Recent Purchases button is a list of artist names, reflecting artists whose music you've purchased. Tap an artist, and you see a listing for any albums by that artist that you've purchased. You can download albums simply by tapping the cloud button next to the album entry. If you want just a track or two from that album, tap a track's name; then, in the resulting screen, tap the cloud button next to the tracks you want. You can also tap the All Songs entry to see all the songs by that artist that you've purchased. Again, you can download individual tracks. Finally, the Download All button is on the artist's screen, and you know what it does.

The TV Shows screen is similar. Tap TV Shows on the Purchased screen, and you see All TV Episodes, Recent Purchases, and then show titles. As you can with music purchases, you can download single episodes or (by tapping a show title) entire seasons.

More

When you tap the More button at the bottom of the screen, you see seven entries: Genius, Ping, Tones, Podcasts, Audiobooks, iTunes U, and Downloads.

Genius

I talk about the Genius feature in Chapter 6. Apple leverages this information to recommend music, movies, and TV shows that you may enjoy. Unlike the Genius feature in iTunes, this one is based not on what's in your iTunes Library, but on what you've purchased from the iTunes Store.

I needn't go through each button and setting. Just know you'll find Music, Movies, and TV Shows buttons. Each entry shows you a thumbnail of the artwork associated with the item, its titles, and a reason for its recommendation—*Based on Patty Griffin,* for example.

Ping

Ping is Apple's music-centric social-networking service. Similar to Facebook, it lets you find people to follow—ideally, those whose musical tastes you respect, but you can just as easily follow your tasteless pals. In turn, other people follow you. Then you recommend or comment on music available from the iTunes Store. (You can't recommend music that's *not* available in the store.)

When you tap Ping, you find that you can choose Activity, People, and My Profile. Activity tells you what the people you're following have been up to. Tapping People shows you a list of the people you follow, as well as those who follow you. (At the bottom of the People screen are buttons labeled Featured, Artists We Recommend You Follow, and People We Recommend You Follow. The latter two buttons are self-explanatory; the Featured button lists the hep and cool.) Finally, My Profile provides a list of all the things you've done on Ping recently.

Tones

This entry was once called Ringtones and was for purchasing 30-second song snippets that would serve as...well, your iPhone's ringtones. Now that the iPhone and iPod touch support customizable alert sounds for just about every function, you can also purchase alert tones. Tapping Tones is the avenue for doing exactly that. Ringtones cost $1.29 each and are based on songs, whereas alert tones are priced at 99 cents each. To preview a ringtone or alert tone, just tap its title.

Podcasts

The Podcasts screen has its own three buttons: What's Hot, Top Tens, and Categories. If you read the sections on the Music and Videos areas earlier in this chapter, you have a solid idea of how this screen works. Podcasts come in both audio and video form, and all of them are free.

Audiobooks

Like Audible.com, the iTunes Store sells audiobooks that you can play on an iPod touch or iPhone, as well as your computer. Like music tracks, audiobooks can be burned to CD.

iTunes U

If you don't already know, iTunes U is the educational area of the store, where you can download lectures, classes, and concerts offered (for the most part) by universities and colleges. Again, iTunes U content is free.

Downloads

The Downloads section bears some scrutiny. As you might expect, this area is where you can watch the progress of the content you're down-loading. It works like this: When you tap a price, it turns into a Buy Now button. Tap that button, and the item swoops down onto the Downloads icon, at which point you're prompted for your iTunes password (the same password that you use at the iTunes Store). Similarly, if you've tapped a cloud button next to a previously purchased item to download it to your device, it too plummets onto the Downloads icon.

An icon on the Downloads button blinks, indicating the number of items that the device is downloading. Tap this icon, and a screen shows you the progress of the download (**Figure 7.2**). After the item has downloaded, you can play it on your device.

Figure 7.2
The Downloads screen lets you watch the progress of music coming to your iPhone or iPod touch.

When these tracks have downloaded for the first time—which would be the case if you've just purchased the music via your iPhone or iPod touch—a new playlist appears below the store heading in the computer-based version of iTunes' Source list. That playlist is called Purchased on *nameofdevice*, where *nameofdevice* is the name you've given your iPhone or iPod touch. After these tracks are in your iTunes Library, they behave like any others you own. You can burn music tracks to disc, and you can play any media on any of your authorized computers or any other iPhones or iPods you may own. If the tracks already exist, and you've simply re-downloaded them via the Purchased screen, they won't appear twice in iTunes on your Mac or PC.

note If an album that you purchase on your device is bundled with extra content (such as a digital booklet and/or videos), when you sync the device with your computer to download the music to it and connect to the iTunes Store, the extra content downloads to iTunes automatically.

Don't Forget Automatic Downloads!

In the old days, you didn't have access to something you downloaded to your iOS device until you synced it with iTunes. With iCloud, that's no longer the case. As I mention in discussing iCloud in Chapter 2, you can have items that you download on your iPhone or iPod touch also download automatically to your other devices—including your computer with iTunes running. Again, to do that, launch Settings, tap Store, and enable Music, Apps, and Books in the Automatic Downloads screen. To ensure that your purchases also download to your computer, open iTunes' preferences window, click Store, and enable the Automatic Downloads options you find there as well.

The App Store

The App Store is a service hosted by Apple that lets you download apps created by Apple and third-party developers to your iPhone, iPod touch, or (via the iTunes Store) computer.

The App Store offers apps that you must pay for as well as scads of free ones, so even the most cheapskate iOS device owners among us will find lots to like at this store. In this section, I show you how it works.

Browsing the App Store

The App Store offers an interface similar to what you find at the iTunes Store. Tap the App Store icon on the Home screen, and along the bottom of the resulting App Store screen, you'll see the five icons necessary to make your shopping experience as enjoyable as possible. The icons break down this way.

Featured

Tap the first icon in the row, and you move to the Featured screen. You'll find three buttons at the top: New, What's Hot, and Genius.

New. Tap New, and you see a list of notable apps—some free, some for sale—that have been added to the App Store recently (**Figure 7.3**).

Figure 7.3
Featured apps from the App Store.

Each entry includes the app's name, its maker, its user review rating (one to five stars), the number of reviews it's received, and its price. At the bottom of this list, you find the now-familiar Redeem and Apple ID entries, which work exactly as they do in the iTunes Store app.

What's Hot. When you tap What's Hot at the top of this screen, you see a list of the most-downloaded apps on the service. Each app bears the same information: name, maker, rating, number of reviews, and price.

Genius. This button operates very much like Apple's Genius playlists. You volunteer to participate by switching Genius on for apps. After you enter your Apple ID password and agree to the terms of service, you see a list of 15 apps, recommended to you based on the other apps that you've purchased from the App Store. To see another 15 recommendations, tap the More Recommendations button at the bottom of the list.

Categories

If you'd like to browse the App Store for particular kinds of apps—games, finance, or productivity, for example—tap the Categories icon that appears in the second position at the bottom of the screen. The Categories screen is where you'll find apps listed in categories, including (at this writing) Games, Newsstand, Entertainment, Utilities, Social Networking, Music, Productivity, Lifestyle, Reference, Travel, Sports, Navigation, Health & Fitness, News, Photo & Video, Finance, Business, Education, Weather, Books, and Medical.

Tap any of these categories except Games, and the resulting category screen includes three buttons that make it easier to find the apps you want: Top Paid, Top Free, and Release Date. When you tap Games, you're offered a screen that includes game genres, much like the one in iTunes. Tap a game genre—Arcade, for example—and you'll see the Top Paid, Top Free, and Release Date buttons, along with a list of 25 games below. Any apps that you've previously purchased but that aren't on your device display an Install button rather than the price of the app. To install the app, simply tap its name, and in the resulting screen, tap Install.

Top 25

Featuring Top Paid, Top Free, and Top Grossing buttons at the top of the screen, Top 25 is what it says—a list of the 25 most-downloaded or most-money-generating apps at the App Store (**Figure 7.4**). Scroll to the bottom of any of these lists to find a Show Top 50 entry. Tap it, and another 25 entries appear, slightly less "top" than the first 25.

Figure 7.4
*A Top 25 screen at
the App Store.*

Search

Search is for those times when you think, "Hmm ... Priscilla said something about a cool new app, but the only part of its name I remember
is *monkey*." Just tap Search, tap in the Search field, and type **monkey** on
the keyboard. You'll be sure to find the app you're after in the list that
appears. Tap the app's name, and you'll see its listing along with the
usual information—name, company, yada, as well as yada.

Updates

Just like the applications you have on your computer, iOS apps are
updated by their developers to fix problems and offer new features.
When an app you've downloaded has been updated—and Apple has
made that update available—the Update icon at the bottom of the
App Store screen bears a red circle with a number inside it, indicating
how many updates are available. The App Store icon on the Home screen
also adopts this icon.

To update your apps over a Wi-Fi or 3G connection, tap the Updates button.
You can update all the apps on your device by tapping Update All, or you

can update them individually by tapping them and then tapping Update on the resulting screen.

 Remember that over 3G, you can download only those apps that are 20 MB and smaller.

Updating Apps on Your Computer

You can also update your apps within iTunes on your Mac or PC. Select Apps in iTunes' Source list, and any apps that you've downloaded from within iTunes (or downloaded on your iPhone or iPod touch and then synced back to iTunes) appear as a series of icons. Click one of these icons, choose File > Get Info, and click the Summary tab in the resulting window, and you'll see how large the app is, its version, who purchased it (and with which account), and the purchase date.

In the bottom-right section of the Apps window are two links: X Updates Available (where X equals the number of available updates for the apps in your iTunes Library) and Get More Apps. Click the first link, and a My App Updates pane appears, listing all the updates available to you. Within this pane, you can download individual updates by clicking the Get Update button next to the app or simply click the Download All Free Updates button in the top-right corner of the pane to download all updates.

After you enter your iTunes password, the updates start downloading. You can check the progress of the downloads by clicking the Downloads entry in the iTunes Store area of iTunes' Source list. When the updates are downloaded, just sync your device to iTunes, and the updated versions of the apps will be copied to your iPhone or iPod touch.

Sharp-eyed readers following along at home will notice a Purchased entry at the top of the Updates screen. Tap it to access previously purchased apps for re-download. The wisest course in this case is to tap Not on This iPhone/iPod rather than All (because there's no need to re-download an app that's already on your device) and then tap the cloud button next to the app you want to download to your device.

When you download an app, your device moves to the Home screen, and the updated version of the app begins to download. The progress of the download is shown in the form of a blue progress bar at the bottom of the updating app's icon.

Managing apps

Now that you've found the apps you're after, you'll want to find out more about them and then start downloading the ones you want.

Navigating the Info screen

An app's Info screen (**Figure 7.5**) is both the gateway to downloading the thing and a source of information about it. Here, you find the name of the app, the name of the developer, a star rating based on user reviews, the number of reviews, a price button that you tap to purchase the app, a link to the reviews, a description and screen shots of the app, contact information for the developer, posting date, version, size, and age-appropriate rating.

Figure 7.5
An app's Info screen.

Tell a Friend and Gift This App (if the app isn't free) buttons also appear in this screen. Tap the first one, and a new unaddressed email message opens, containing the name of the app in the Subject field and the words *Check out this application:* followed by a link to the app in the message body. The recipient of this message need only click the link; as long as she has a current copy of iTunes installed on her computer, iTunes will launch and take her to the iTunes Store page that's devoted to this app. (I discuss the iTunes Store's relationship with apps shortly.)

When you tap Gift This App, you see a screen of the same name that includes all the information about the app, plus Next and Cancel buttons. Tap Next, and the resulting screen provides fields for your name, the recipient's name, the recipient's email address, and an area for creating a personal message (such as "I know you'll love this!"). Fill in these fields, and a confirmation screen appears, letting you double-check that you're sending the right app to the right person. When you're sure that the information is correct, tap the Buy Gift button at the bottom of the screen. An email message with a link to the app will be sent to the recipient, and you'll be charged for the app.

You may also see an App Support button on this screen. (As I write this chapter, it doesn't appear on every app screen.) The idea is that if you need help with an app, you tap this button. Safari will launch and take you to the support page of the developer's Web site.

Reviews work similarly to the reviews for music in the iTunes app. The difference is that you're not allowed to review an app unless you've actually downloaded it, which helps prevent useless "This costs too much!" or "I hate cheese!" reviews that can drag down an app's rating.

Finally, there's the Report a Problem button. Tap it, and a Report a Problem screen appears, offering three choices: The Application Has a Bug, This Application Is Offensive, and My Concern Is Not Listed Here.

These choices are followed by a Comments field where you can express yourself more thoroughly. Tap Report to send your report to Apple.

Downloading apps

Tap the entry for the app you want to download. Tap its price (yes, even if it's marked Free) and then tap Install. You'll be prompted for, at the very least, your iTunes password. I say *at least* because if you were signed in to the iTunes Store the last time you synced your iPhone or iPod touch, you won't be prompted for your iTunes account when you attempt to download something from the App Store. If you're using the App Store for the first time and aren't signed in to your iTunes account within iTunes, you'll be prompted for both your account address and password.

Enter your password with the keyboard, and tap OK. The device moves to the Home screen, shows a dimmed icon for the app you're downloading, and displays Loading and then Installing progress bars at the bottom of the screen. When the app is fully loaded, the Installing progress bar disappears, and the icon takes on its full color and brightness. To launch the app, do as you do with any app on the device: Tap its icon.

tip If you've run out of patience waiting for a particularly hefty app to finish downloading, you can pause the download simply by tapping its icon. If another app is in the update queue, it begins downloading instead. To resume downloading the first app, just tap its icon on the Home screen.

Again, if you've enabled automatic downloads on both your device and computer, any apps that you obtain with your iPhone or iPod touch also download to your other devices.

iBooks and the iBookstore

You've likely heard about Apple's iPad, the slatelike computing device that some people have compared with a large iPod touch. In addition to being a great media player, though, the iPad is a darned good e-book reader. The means for getting e-books onto the iPad is Apple's free iBooks app. This app—designed for reading e-books and PDF files as well as downloading e-books—turned out to be so popular that Apple took the next logical step and offered it to iPhones and iPod touches running iOS 4 and later. In this section, I look at how it works on these devices.

Getting iBooks

Before you can visit the iBookstore, you need to have a copy of iBooks on your iPhone or iPod touch. Apple doesn't install it by default, so you must download it, which is easy to do because the first time you launch the App Store, you'll be asked whether you'd like to download it. Reply in the affirmative and enter your Apple ID password, and iBooks will soon be on your device.

Browsing the iBookstore

To obtain books from the iBookstore, launch the iBooks app, and tap the Store button in the top-right corner of the display. When you do, the virtual bookshelf flips around and takes you to the iBookstore (**Figure 7.6**).

Like the iTunes and App stores, the iBookstore features the now-familiar five icons along the bottom of the screen. In this case, those icons are Featured, Charts, Browse, Search, and Purchased. They break out this way.

Figure 7.6
*Apple's virtual
bookstore.*

Featured

Tap Featured, and you see a screen that includes (as I write this chapter)
four banners, which promote specific titles and special offers and collections. Below the banners is a New & Notable section that lists new and
popular titles.

In the top-left corner is a Categories button. Tap it, and up scrolls a list
of book categories (analogous to the iTunes Store's Genres section). Tap
a category, and you're taken to that category's screen, where books are
listed below a New & Notable heading. To return to the main Featured
screen, tap Categories again; then select All.

Charts

The Charts screen lets you browse the iBookstore's hot titles, as well as
books featured in *The New York Times*' best-selling fiction and nonfiction
lists. To see the big sellers at the iBookstore, tap Top Charts. Below, you'll
find the top ten paid and top ten free titles. Below each list is a Ten More
Books entry that, when tapped, shows you exactly that. Tap the New York

Times button, and you see lists of the ten top fiction and ten top nonfiction titles, along with the Ten More Books entries for each list.

A Categories button appears in this screen as well. Tap it, and you'll view the top-charting e-books for the category you choose (Arts & Entertainment, Classics, or Fiction & Literature, for example).

Browse

Tap Browse, and you're presented with an Authors screen, with Top Paid and Top Free buttons adorning the top. Below is an alphabetical list of authors. Just find an author whose work you want to explore and then tap his or her name; a list of available books appears.

Search

You've searched for something on your iPhone or iPod touch or within one of the stores by now, right? Same idea here. Tap the Search field, type a keyword, and then tap the Search button. Choose what you like by tapping it in the list of search results.

Purchased

Yes, you can re-download e-books too. Just tap the Purchased screen, and you'll see the now-familiar All and Not on This iPhone/iPod buttons. Choose the latter button and then tap the cloud icon next to the item you want to download to your device.

Downloading and syncing books

Now that you have iBooks on your iPod and have a notion of where to find things, you're ready to download a free book. The iBookstore has lots of free classic, so to download one now, just follow these steps:

1. Tap Search.

2. Enter **study in scarlet** with the keyboard, and tap *A Study in Scarlet* (the first Sherlock Holmes novel) in the results list.

3. In the screen that appears, tap *A Study in Scarlet* (the free version). The book's page in the iBookstore opens.

4. Tap the Free button, which changes to Get Book; then tap Get Book.

5. Sign in or enter your Apple ID and password when you're prompted to do so.

   The screen flips around to reveal the image of a wooden bookshelf, and the cover of *A Study in Scarlet* appears on the top shelf with an embedded progress bar. When the bar disappears, the book is ready to read, bearing a New banner across the top-right corner. (Free books often have generic covers. Books that you pay for have more interesting covers.)

   If you've switched on automatic downloads on your computer, the book also download to your Mac or PC if iTunes is running. If you haven't enabled this option when you next sync your device, this book and any others that you've obtained on your iPhone or iPod touch will be copied to your iTunes Library and will appear when you select Books in iTunes' Source list.

> **tip** The iBookstore isn't the only way to get books on your device. You can also drag ePub- and PDF-formatted documents into iTunes. Do that, and the files appear in iTunes' Books pane, ready for you to sync to the device.

Reading books with iBooks

Reading a book or PDF with iBooks couldn't be much easier. Just launch the iBooks app, and by default, you see a bookshelf populated with the e-book titles you've downloaded. If you've also synced PDF files to iBooks (by adding them to iTunes), you can see them by tapping the PDFs button at the top of the screen.

If the bookshelf-as-interface thing doesn't work for you because you've synced a lot of books or PDFs to your device, tap and flick down the display. A Search field appears, along with Cover and List View icons. Tap the List View icon to see titles arranged in a list. When you view titles in a list, four sorting buttons appear at the bottom of the screen: Bookshelf, Titles, Authors, and Categories. Tap one, and the titles will be sorted by this criterion.

To read a book or PDF file, just tap its icon. The book or PDF zooms to the fore and displays the first page (which, in the case of e-book files, is often the cover page). To turn pages, just flick from the right side of the screen to the left or tap the right side of the display. To back up a page, flick from left to right or tap the left side of the screen. To move to a specific page, drag the page slider at the bottom of the screen. When you do, a small window appears that tells you the chapter name as well as the page number you've slid to. At the very bottom of the screen, you see a page-number indicator—*74 of 305*, for example. When you're reading an e-book, you also see the number of pages left in the book. With PDF files, small thumbnail images of the PDF appear at the bottom of the screen.

At the top of the screen, you see the series of buttons shown in **Figure 7.7**.

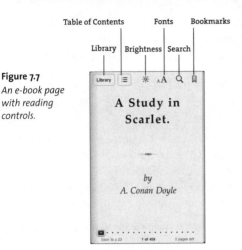

Figure 7.7
*An e-book page
with reading
controls.*

Table of Contents   Fonts   Bookmarks

Library | Brightness | Search

Here's how to use each button:

- **Library.** Tap this button to return to the list of all the books or PDFs in your device's library.

- **Table of Contents.** Tap this button, and you see a screen that displays the book's table of contents, if it has one. (Not all books include a table of contents, and no PDFs do.) Tap a chapter in the table of contents to go to the beginning of that chapter. This screen also contains a Bookmarks button. When you tap it, you see a list of any bookmarks you've added to the book or PDF you're reading. (I show you how to add bookmarks later in this section.) To return to reading the book, tap the Resume button at the top of the screen.

- **Brightness.** The iBooks app allows you to adjust the device's brightness independently. This feature is terrific for those times when you don't want to disturb your bedmate with a bright light when she's trying to sleep and you're hoping to read. Just tap this button and drag the Brightness slider to make the adjustment.

- **Fonts.** The next button, Fonts, lets you change the size of an e-book's text, the fonts it uses, and whether you see a white or sepia page. (The Fonts button doesn't appear when you tap the PDF button, as you can't change a PDF's font or font size.) The small and large *A* buttons allow you to choose the size of the text in nine increments—from you-will-never-need-glasses-in-your-entire-life Lilliputian to Coke-bottle-bottom-glasses gigantic.

  You can also choose a font: Baskerville, Cochin, Georgia, Palatino, Times New Roman, or Verdana. All but Verdana attempt to replicate the serif fonts used in most paper books; Verdana looks far more "computery," with its sans-serif appearance. Also, a Sepia On/Off toggle lets you change the color of the page from white to slightly brown.

- **Search.** Tap the Search button, and you have the option to search not only the contents of the book or PDF, but also Google and Wikipedia. When you search for contents within a book or PDF, iBooks is quite literal. Suppose that you're reading *Winnie-the-Pooh* (which was once offered for free). If you tap the Search field and enter **winnie-the-pooh bees**, you receive no results. Enter **winnie-the-pooh and some bees**, however, and you get two results—pages in the introduction and in Chapter 1—because that exact phrase appears on those pages.

  If you care to search farther afield, tap either the Search Google or Search Wikipedia button at the bottom of the screen. Each button launches the Safari app and takes you to the related Web site, where you see the results of your search. To return to iBooks from such a search, just double-click the Home button and tap the iBooks icon in the resulting Dock.

- **Bookmarks.** Earlier, I promised to tell you how to bookmark pages in a book or PDF. As it turns out, the process is only as complicated as tapping the Bookmarks button at the top of the screen. Do so, and a red book-mark appears on the currently displayed page. When you page through the book in the future, you'll see this red mark on each bookmarked page. To delete a bookmark, simply tap it, and it disappears. As I mentioned very recently, to find a list of all your bookmarks, just tap the Table of Contents button and then tap Bookmarks on the resulting screen.

Setting in-book options

When you tap and hold a word in an e-book, a gray bubble appears, offering four or five options: Copy, Dictionary, Highlight, Note, and Search (**Figure 7.8**). (These options don't appear for PDFs.)

Figure 7.8
An e-book's in-book options.

The in-book options work this way:

- **Copy.** This option appears when you select words in an unprotected e-book, such as the free e-books available from the iBookstore and Project Gutenberg (www.gutenberg.org). (You can't copy text from the retail e-books sold at the iBookstore.) Copy does just what it does in any other iOS app—copies the word or selection to the iPhone's or iPod touch's clipboard. Then you can paste the text into a different app, such as Notes, or into a email message.

- **Dictionary.** The iBooks app includes a built-in dictionary. When you stumble upon the word *dirigible,* for example, and need to know its meaning, just highlight the word and then tap Dictionary.

- **Highlight.** Some people love nothing better than marking up their paper books with a yellow highlighter. This command offers the electronic equivalent.

- **Note.** If highlighting just won't do the trick, and you prefer to jot notes in the margins instead, this button is the way. Tap Note, and a yellow field appears, along with the device's keyboard. Type your note and tap Done, and a Note icon appears in the book's margin. Tap the icon to edit or read the note.

- **Search.** When you want to find every instance of the name *Voldemort* in your electronic copy of *Harry Potter and the Deathly Hallows*, you may be surprised to discover that He-Who-Must-Not-Be-Named is named several hundred times in the text. Results include not only the page on which the term or phrase was found, but also a snippet of text in which the term appears.

8

Photos, Camera, and YouTube

iOS devices are audio wonders, playing music when called upon to do so. But they're also visual delights—and no, I'm not referring to their lustrous design. I'm talking pictures (both those you take and those you view), the moving pictures you can record with a 4G iPod touch, iPhone 4, or iPhone 4S; and those streamed from the free Web-based video-sharing service YouTube.

In this chapter, I turn to the visual: the iPhone's and iPod touch's photo, camera, and YouTube capabilities.

You Ought to Be in Pictures

Tapping Photos in the iPhone's or iPod touch's Home screen is the digital equivalent of flipping open your wallet to reveal a seemingly endless stream of pictures of the kids, the dog, and that recent trip to Coober Pedy. The Photos app, however, is no mere repository for pictures. Flick a finger, and you're flying from photo to photo. Spread your fingers, and you've zoomed in on a picture's most poignant portion. If you have a more formal presentation in mind—a showing of your child's first birthday party for Grandma and Grandpa, for example—you can create something far grander in the form of a slideshow. And if you have movies in your Mac's iPhoto library, the Photos app can play those too. To find out about these and other visual wonders, just follow along.

Seeing the face of Photos: Albums

When you tap Photos, you see the Albums screen, which acts as the gateway to the images stored on your camera (**Figure 8.1**). In this screen, you'll find at least one entry, and there'll be more after you sync photos to your device. You'll also see three or four icons at the bottom of the display: Albums, Events, Faces, and Places. As I discuss in Chapter 2, the version of Photos that comes with iOS 4 and iOS 5 includes support for iPhoto's Events, Faces, and Places features.

Figure 8.1
The Albums screen.

note Why the uncertainty about how many icons adorn the bottom of the screen? If you haven't synced images with Faces information, the Faces icon won't appear.

The first entry is Camera Roll. Tap it to see the images you've captured by using the iPhone's or iPod touch's camera or screen-capture shortcut (hold the Home button while quickly pressing the Sleep/Wake button), the images that have been sent to you by email, the images that have come to your device via iCloud's Photo Stream, and the images you've copied from Safari.

To the left of this entry in the Albums screen, you'll see a thumbnail image of the last picture added to the album. To the right of the entry, in parentheses, you'll see the combined number of images that this album contains—*Camera Roll (374),* for example. The > character at the far-right edge of the screen indicates that when you tap this entry, you'll be taken to another screen. That other screen, called Camera Roll, contains thumbnail images of all the photos, movies, and screenshots in this album.

The next entry, Photo Stream, appears if you have an iCloud account and you've enabled the Photo Stream option in the iCloud settings screen. As I explain when talking about iCloud in Chapter 2, when you activate this option on your iOS devices, any pictures you capture are distributed automatically among all your devices. So when you shoot a picture with your iPhone, it also appears on your iPod touch (provided that you've enabled Photo Stream on that device as well).

Next comes Photo Library, which contains all the photos on your device save for those in the Camera Roll. It too bears a thumbnail (not one of your images, but a sunflower), and it displays the total number of images in the library—*Photo Library (81),* for example. Tap this entry, and in the resulting Photo Library screen, you'll see thumbnail images of all the photos on your device (again, excluding the Camera Roll images).

As you see in Chapter 2, you can sync photo albums created by such programs as iPhoto, Aperture, Adobe Photoshop Elements, and Adobe Photoshop Albums. When you do, these albums appear in the Albums screen as separate entries, each featuring a thumbnail of the first image in the album as well as the number of images in the album—*Father's Day (48)* or *Family Holiday (92)*, for example.

When you select your Pictures folder (Mac, Windows Vista, and Windows 7), My Pictures (Windows XP), or a folder of your choosing within iTunes' Photos tab, any folders contained in those folders are presented as separate albums. So, for example, if your Pictures folder holds three folders that contain pictures—say, *Betty's Birthday*, *Dog Polisher*, and *Cheeses Loved and Lost*—each of those items appears as a separate album in the Albums screen. Again, each album lists the number of images it contains in parentheses.

If you're a Mac user and store your pictures in iPhoto '09 or iPhoto '11, you're probably aware that iPhoto automatically groups pictures taken during the same general period into events—a single day, for example. In the Photos tab within iTunes, you can ask that iPhoto's 1, 3, 5, 10, or 20 most recent events be synced to your device (**Figure 8.2**). You can view those events by tapping the Events icon at the bottom of the Albums screen.

Additionally, in recent versions of iTunes, you can sync Faces and Places albums to your device (as I explain in Chapter 2). Again, you can access these images by tapping the Faces and Places icons at the bottom of the screen.

Figure 8.2
Sync iPhoto's most recent events to your iPhone or iPod touch.

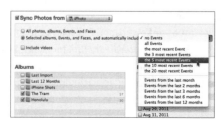

iPhoto users have one additional advantage: When you connect a 4G iPod touch, 5G iPod nano, iPhone 3GS, iPhone 4, or iPhone 4S, iPhoto offers to import that device's video. I explain the mechanics of this process in "Syncing photos and videos to your computer" later in this chapter.

Working with the Photos app

As I mention earlier in this chapter, when you're in an Albums screen, you see all the pictures in that album arrayed four across as thumbnail images (**Figure 8.3**). You can see 20 thumbnails onscreen. If your album contains more than 20 images, just flick your finger up across the display to scroll more images into view. To see a picture or movie full-screen, just tap it.

Figure 8.3
A photo album's
thumbnail
images.

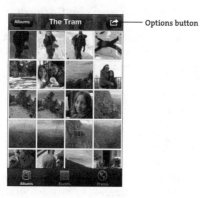

Options button

From this thumbnails screen, you can also copy pictures and movies. To do that, just tap and hold the picture or movie you want to copy. A Copy bubble appears. Tap it, and the item is copied to the device's clipboard.

Currently, the iPhone's and iPod touch's Mail app is the only Apple app that lets you paste images and movies.

Setting thumbnail-screen options

You know that when you tap the name of an album, that album appears with its contents displayed as thumbnails. In the top-right corner of the album screen, you see an Options button (refer to Figure 8.3). Tap this button to view a Select Items screen (called Select Photos if there are no movies in the album). If you've accessed this screen from any album other than Camera Roll, you'll see three buttons: Share, Copy, and Add To. Tap the Options button within the Camera Roll album, and you see one additional button: Delete.

Location and the Camera

By default, your 4G iPod touch, iPhone 4, or iPhone 4S *geotags* photos and videos shot with its camera—meaning that it embeds location data in each photo and video it shoots. So if you take a few pictures with your iPhone or iPod touch, launch the Photos app, and then tap the Places button, you should see a map with a red pin that points to the place where you took those photos.

Tap the pin, and a gray bubble appears. This bubble displays a thumbnail image of the first item in the photo library; the number of pictures and videos taken at that location (*7 photos,* for example); and a blue > icon that, when tapped, takes you to a screen that includes thumbnails of the images and movies shot at that location. Tap a thumbnail to view the image or movie.

If you'd rather not have location information added to your images and movies, travel to Settings > Location Services, and toggle the Camera entry's On/Off switch to Off.

The buttons work this way:

- **Share.** Tap one or more images and then tap Share, and three or four buttons scroll up from the bottom of the screen. Four buttons—Email, Message, Print, and Cancel—appear if you select more than one item. If you select a single item, a Tweet button is added to the mix. And if you select a movie and tap the Share button, your options are Email, Message, Send to YouTube, and Cancel.

  When you tap Send to YouTube, a Publish Video screen appears. If you haven't yet signed in to YouTube within the Photos app, you'll be prompted for your YouTube user name and password. After entering that information and tapping Sign In, you'll need to enter a title, description, and tags for your movie, as well as choose a category from a pop-up menu (Comedy, Gaming, or Sports, for example). Tap Publish, and your movie is uploaded to YouTube.

- **Email** does what you'd expect. When you tap this button, the selected images are imported into an empty email message. Just fill in the recipient and add a Subject line, and you're ready to send.

- **Tweet** is for attaching the image to a Twitter message. Tap this button, and if you don't have a Twitter account configured, you'll be prompted to enter your Twitter user name and password in the Twitter settings screen. If you've already configured Twitter, tap this button, and a tweet that contains the image is created. Add some text, and tap Send.

- **Message** is likewise an intuitive command. Tap it, and the Messages app opens, with the image attached as part of a media message, Just fill in the To field; type some text to accompany your image, if you like; and tap Send.

- **Print** is, of course, for printing the image to a compatible printer. I discuss printing in Chapter 10.

- **Cancel** delivers on that promise.

- **Copy.** Tap this option, and the selected images and/or movies are copied to the device's clipboard. Then you can paste them into compatible apps (see "Viewing pictures" and "Viewing movies" later in this chapter).

- **Add To.** This command, introduced with iOS 5, allows you to select images and add them to a new or existing album. The first time you tap Add To, you'll be offered only the choice to add photos to a new album. After you've created that new album, subsequent taps allow you to add images to one of the albums you created with the Add To button.

- **Delete.** Select images and/or movies within the Camera Roll album and tap Delete, and they're removed.

Setting picture-screen options

When you tap a thumbnail image, you see that image and, briefly, a gray bar along the bottom that contains two or three icons: Options, Play, and possibly Trash. (Trash appears only when you view images in the Camera Roll.) Tap Play, and a slideshow starts. Trash is equally intuitive; it deletes the current image or movie. Options, however, presents a few choices that aren't available in an album's thumbnails screen.

When you tap Options, the bottom of the screen rolls up to display seven or eight buttons: Email Photo, Message, Assign to Contact, Use As Wallpaper, Tweet, Print, Save to Camera Roll, and Cancel (**Figure 8.4**). The wildcard is the Save to Camera Roll button that appears when you select an image in the Photo Stream album.

Figure 8.4
*Options available
in a picture
screen.*

Email Photo

Message

Assign to Contact

Use as Wallpaper

Tweet

Print

Cancel

You know what Email Photo, Message, Tweet, Print, and Cancel do. As for
the others:

- **Assign to Contact.** You may recall that you can assign pictures to
  the names in the Contacts app. This button is one other avenue for
  doing that.

- **Use As Wallpaper.** When your iPhone's or iPod touch's screen goes
  black, it hasn't turned itself off; rather, it locked itself and switched off
  the screen to save power. When you click the Home button to bring the
  screen back to life, you see the Lock screen. On this screen is an image
  called wallpaper; the Home screen's background image is also wallpaper. So what you're doing here is telling the device that you'd like
  to use the current image as a wallpaper background. Tap this button,
  and you can move and scale the image, using pinch and drag gestures.
  When you're ready to use the image, tap Set. You'll be prompted to
  choose how you want the image to be used: Set Lock Screen, Set Home
  Screen, Set Both, or Cancel. Tap the option you want.

- **Save to Camera Roll.** Tap this option when you're viewing an image in
  the Photo Stream album, and that image will be copied exactly where
  promised.

Editing pictures

Why, yes, thanks to iOS 5 you can now edit images directly on the iPhone or iPod touch. Why, no, you're not getting the capabilities offered by Adobe Photoshop or even iPhoto. Instead, you're allowed to perform some very basic edits. Tap an image and then tap the Edit button in the top-right corner. At the bottom of the screen are four buttons: Rotate, Auto Enhance, Remove Red Eye, and Crop (**Figure 8.5**).

Figure 8.5
The Photos app's editing tools.

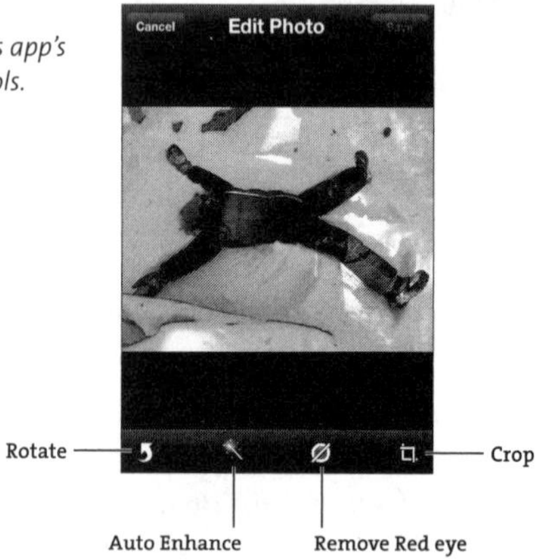

Rotate — Crop

Auto Enhance — Remove Red eye

The icons work this way:

Rotate. Tap the Rotate button, and the image flips 90 degrees counterclockwise.

Auto Enhance. Tap this button, and the device attempts to improve the image by adjusting brightness, contrast, and color saturation.

Remove Red Eye. If the people in your pictures exhibit vampirelike red eyes, you can attempt to remove that unhealthy cast. To do so, zoom in on a red eye by using the stretch gesture and then tap where you find the red. The area should turn black. (If Photos can't find any red, a message appears, telling you so.) If you're happy with the results, tap the Apply button in the top-right corner of the screen. If you don't like the results, tap the eye again to undo the effect.

Crop. If you'd like to cut out the cruft in a photo, tap the Crop button. This button shrinks the image so that you can see all of it and impose a grid (**Figure 8.6**). Just tap and drag a corner or side to resize the image. Tap Crop to do that. If you're pleased with what you've done, tap Save; if not, tap Cancel.

Figure 8.6
*Cropping images
in the Photos app.*

note When you tap Crop, you see a Constrain button at the bottom of the screen. Tap that button, and you'll discover that you can choose among a variety of crop ratios.

Viewing pictures

Navigating through your pictures is as simple as swiping your finger to the left to advance to the next picture or to the right to retreat one picture. Now try this: Double-tap an interesting spot in a picture. Like magic, the screen zooms and places that spot as close to the center of the screen as it can. Drag your finger on the picture to reposition it. If you'd like greater control of how large the image is, use the spread gesture (which I discuss in Chapter 1) to make it grow incrementally.

Swiping is good at any time, even during a slideshow. If, while viewing a slideshow, you'd like to take control, just tap the display to stop the slideshow, or swipe your finger to the left to advance or to the right to go back. When you manually navigate to the photo that precedes or follows the one on view, the slideshow is canceled. To restart it, just tap the screen to make the control bar appear, and tap the Play icon.

These settings are the defaults. If you've configured the Photos settings so that the Repeat and Shuffle options are on, the slideshow behaves a bit differently. To begin with, when the show reaches the end, it starts over, continuing to play until you tell it to stop by tapping the display. And if Shuffle is on, the photos in the selected album play in random order.

If you've viewing the contents of the Camera Roll album, it's likely that you'll encounter a movie or two that you've taken with your device. I cover viewing movies in the next section.

Viewing movies

When you tap a movie in the Camera Roll or one within an album that you've synced to the device, you see an interface seemingly identical to what you're accustomed to seeing for pictures. At the bottom of this screen are four or five buttons: Options, Play, AirPlay, and (if you're viewing the movie within the Camera Roll screen) Trash.

Tap Options, and a screen rolls up that reveals Email Video, Message, Send to YouTube, and Cancel buttons. These options (excluding Send to YouTube, which isn't an option for pictures) work just as they do for images you export via similar buttons.

To play the movie, tap either the Play icon at the bottom of the screen or the larger Play icon in the middle of the screen. When you tap either icon, the Play icon at the bottom of the screen changes to Pause. Tap AirPlay, and a menu scrolls up, displaying any AirPlay-compatible devices you have (an Apple TV, for example), which your iPhone or iPod touch can then stream video to.

Along the top of the screen is a series of thumbnail images (**Figure 8.7**), which is the movie timeline. On this timeline is a narrow silver playhead. To navigate quickly through the movie—forward or backward—just drag the playhead. You can also edit the movie by using this timeline, as I discuss in the "Playing and editing video" section later in the chapter.

Figure 8.7
Viewing a movie in the Photos app.

You can get much finer control by tapping and holding the playhead. When you do, the timeline expands to show a subset of the thumbnail images closest to the playhead.

Snapping Pictures

The 4G iPod touch, iPhone 4, and iPhone 4S have two cameras: one on the back and another on the front. Although the 4G iPod touch is similar in form to the iPhone 4 and 4S, its rear-facing camera isn't nearly as good as the one on the iPhones. The iPhone 4S's 8-megapixel camera captures still images at a resolution of 3264 x 2448 pixels, the iPhone 4's 5-megapixel camera shoots stills at a resolution of 2592 x 1936 pixels, and the iPod touch's 0.7-megapixel rear-facing back camera captures JPEG images at a resolution of just 720 x 960 pixels—definitely poorer results than either of the iPhones. All these devices include a 5x digital zoom.

These devices can also shoot video. The rear-facing camera on the iPhone 4 and 4G iPod touch can shoot 720p HD movies (1280 x 720 pixels), and the iPhone 4S shoots 1080p video (1920 x 1080 pixels) from this camera. The front-facing camera produces lower resolution on all these devices, shooting JPEG still images at 640 x 480 pixels.

The iPhone 4S introduces changes to the camera other than an increased megapixel specification that improves images. It sports a five-element lens, better aperture (f2.4 versus f2.8 in the iPhone 4, which means better low-light shooting), video stabilization, noise reduction, and face recognition. *Face recognition* means that the camera understands what a face is and automatically adjusts its settings so that the face looks as good as possible compared with the background.

Taking a photo

You have two ways to access the Camera app. The "normal" way is to simply tap the Camera app on the Home screen. In a short time, you see the image of a closed shutter and then a view of whatever's in front of the rear-facing camera lens. The new iOS 5 way is to shoot directly from the device's lock screen—handy when your device is sleeping and you want to grab a quick shot. In this case, just press the Home button twice in succession and then tap the camera icon that appears on the lock screen.

The first time you launch the Camera app, it asks permission to use location information. It does this so that it can embed location information in the picture data—a process called *geotagging*. That way, should you later want to know where you were when you captured that breathtaking shot of the jelly doughnut, you can look up that information in a photo-editing program. You don't have to allow the camera to use location information, however. If you tell the app no, it will still work; you just won't have location information attached to the pictures you take.

note This geotagging business works only if you have Location Services switched on. I mention this option in Chapter 2, but you needn't flip back to find it; it's in Location Services within the Settings app.

Checking out the Camera app

The interface of the Camera app is simple. In the bottom-left corner of the display is a small thumbnail image. Tap it, and you're taken to the Camera Roll screen, where you view the last image captured by the device. Tap the Camera icon in the bottom-left corner to return to the camera interface.

A single Camera button appears at the bottom of the display. The orientation of this button changes based on the orientation of the device: landscape or portrait. A Camera/Video toggle switch appears in the bottom-right corner. Tap this switch to go from taking still pictures to taking movies, and vice versa. In the top-right corner is the Choose Camera button. Tap this button to flip between the rear- and front-facing cameras.

An Options button appears at the top of the screen. Tap that button on an iPhone 4 and iPhone 4S, and you'll find On/Off switches for Grid and HDR. The 4G iPod touch displays only Grid. Switch on Grid, and that's exactly what you see: a tic-tac-toe overlay that helps you line up your shots. HDR (High Dynamic Range) is a scheme whereby the camera combines three exposures of an image to produce one image that combines the best results of the three—say, the deep blue of the sky in one image, the lush green of the rolling hills in another, and your sweetie's adorable mug in yet another (**Figure 8.8**).

Finally, the iPhone 4 and iPhone 4S feature a Flash button for controlling the LED flash on the back of the phone. Your options are Auto (the phone decides when it needs the flash), On (always on regardless of the lighting conditions), and Off. Because the iPod touch doesn't have a flash, this option is absent.

Figure 8.8
The Camera app's interface on an iPhone 4S.

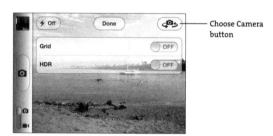

Choose Camera button

Focusing your shot

When you open the Camera app on your device and point it, a box appears onscreen. This box is the iPhone's or iPod touch's way of saying, "I believe that what I've placed in this box is the subject of this picture. My belief is so strong, in fact, that I will focus on this object and adjust my exposure to help it stand out."

If you agree with the device's assessment, you have two ways to take the picture: You can tap the Camera button or press the Volume Up switch on the side of the device. If, however, you want the thing to focus on some other object—say, the flower before you instead of the building behind it—just tap the object that you prefer. The box is drawn around that object instead, and the device adjusts its focus and exposure accordingly.

tip Note the word *exposure*. This box isn't simply for focusing. If you're shooting a landscape, for example, and the brightness of the sky is washing out the scene, tap the sky. The device adjusts the image so that the sky is the subject and, thus, makes the sky darker.

Zooming before shooting

You know how you can zoom in on Safari pages and images in the Photos app just by spreading two fingers? That's exactly how the zoom feature works in iOS 5. Just spread and pinch to zoom in and out, respectively. When you do, a small bar appears at the bottom of the screen, featuring plus (+) and minus (–) buttons on either end. You can tap these buttons to zoom in and out, as well as drag a round controller in the middle of the bar to zoom.

note This feature is available only for still photos. You don't have the option to use zoom when you're shooting a movie.

YouTube

YouTube remains the Big Cheese for watching politicians kill their careers with a few ill-chosen words or photos, frat boys set themselves on fire, and felines impersonate Elvis. Because YouTube is so popular, it only makes sense that the iPhone and iPod touch offer you a way to watch its content. They do so via the YouTube app.

Navigating YouTube

Tap the YouTube icon on the Home screen, and you'll see an interface very much like the one in the Videos app. Like the Videos screen, this one has five buttons along the bottom. By default, these buttons are Featured, Most Viewed, Search, Favorites, and the ever-popular More (**Figure 8.9**).

Figure 8.9
Buttons at the bottom of the YouTube screen.

Here's what you'll find when you tap each button.

Featured

Tap Featured, and you get a list of videos that YouTube believes most worthy of your attention (**Figure 8.10**). To play one, just tap it. The video streams to your device via a Wi-Fi connection. (If your iPhone or iPod touch isn't connected to the Internet, of course, you'll see nothing at all.) When you scroll to the bottom of the list, you'll see a Load More entry. Tap it, and more videos are added to the list.

Figure 8.10
Featured YouTube videos.

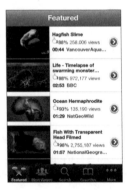

If a video's title, such as *Simon's Cat 'Let Me In!',* doesn't provide you enough information, feel free to tap the blue > icon to the right of the video's title. When you do, you'll see the name of the movie you selected at the top of the screen and three buttons below: Add to Favorites, Add to Playlist, and Share Video.

Tap Add to Favorites, and that video is added to your list of favorites, making it easy to find it again. (I reveal more about favorites shortly.)

You can create playlists of YouTube videos via an option in the More screen. When you tap Add to Playlist, you can choose a playlist to add a video to. Alternatively, tap the plus button in the Add to Playlist screen to create a playlist right then and there.

When you tap Share Video, you see three options (plus Cancel): Add to Favorites, Mail Link to This Video, and Tweet. Choose Mail Link to This Video, and a new email message opens. The Subject line includes the title of the video, and the message body contains *Check out this video on YouTube:*, followed by a link to the video. (You can edit *Check out this video on YouTube:* to anything you like.) When you complete the To field and tap Send, the email message is sent via your default email account (as configured in the Mail settings screen).

The description screen also includes a Related Videos area. If YouTube has videos that it believes are similar in theme to the one you've chosen, it lists them here.

Tap yet another blue > icon to the right of the movie in this screen, and you arrive at the movie's More Info screen (**Figure 8.11**). This screen includes a description of the video; the date when it was added; its category (Drama or Documentary, for example); its tags, which include anything that the poster thought appropriate, such as *poodle*, *waterslide*, and *ointment*; a Rate, Comment, or Flag button for doing just that; and user comments below. To read more comments, tap the Load More Comments button at the bottom of the screen.

If you're interested in seeing other videos uploaded by the producer of the video you're currently exploring, tap the More Videos button at the top of the More Info screen.

Figure 8.11
A YouTube More Info screen.

Most Viewed

The Most Viewed button provides you the opportunity to view YouTube's most popular videos—all videos, or the most viewed today or this week. Like the Featured screen, this one carries a Load More entry at the bottom of the list. To watch all, today's most viewed, or this week's most viewed videos, tap the appropriate button at the top of the screen.

Search

You can search YouTube's catalog of videos, of course, and this button is the way to go about it. Tap Search, and you get a Search field in return. Tap this field, and up pops the keyboard. Type a search term—*skateboard* or *Mentos,* for example—and YouTube searches for videos that match your query. Then it presents a list of 25 videos that it feels match what you're after. If more than 25 videos are available that match your query, your friend the Load More entry appears at the bottom of the list.

Favorites

As the name hints, the Favorites screen (**Figure 8.12**) is where you store links to your favorite YouTube videos. To begin streaming one of these videos, just tap its name.

Figure 8.12
YouTube favorites.

To remove a favorite, tap the Edit button at the top of the screen, tap the red minus button that appears next to the entry, and then tap Delete. When you're finished removing favorites, tap Done to return to the Favorites screen.

> **tip** When you sign in to your YouTube account and add a favorite, that favorite appears not only on your iPhone or iPod touch, but also within YouTube in your computer's Web browser.

More

By now, the More button should be no mystery to you. Tap it, and you get additional choices: Most Recent, Top Rated, History, My Videos, Subscriptions, and Playlists.

Most Recent offers a glimpse of the 25 videos most recently added by YouTube, and Top Rated displays YouTube's 25 highest-rated videos: Today, This Week, or All.

History details all the videos you've chosen. Yes, *chosen*. You don't have to watch these videos for them to appear in your History list. Just choose them, and even if you cancel playback before they appear, they'll be part of your YouTube history. If this list is too long, or if you're embarrassed by some of the things you've chosen, tap the Clear button at the top of the screen. All history entries disappear.

note The Clear button is an all-or-nothing affair. Currently, the iPhone and iPod touch don't provide an option to delete individual videos from the History screen.

My Videos lists all the videos you've uploaded to YouTube under your account.

Subscriptions presents a list of the producers or channels you've subscribed to. The number of videos available in a subscription appears next to its name—*Macworld (324)*, for example.

Finally, as I mention earlier, you can create playlists of YouTube videos. To create a playlist, tap the Edit button in the Playlists screen; then tap the plus button in the top-left corner of the resulting screen. An Add Playlist screen scrolls up from the bottom. Use the keyboard to name your playlist, and tap the Add button when you're done. You can remove playlists later by tapping the Edit button in the Playlists screen and using the tap-minus-and-then-Delete technique.

Playing YouTube videos

To play a YouTube video, tap it, and the video begins loading in landscape orientation. You'll see the now-familiar video play controls—Back, Play, and Next—along with a volume slider, timeline, and Scale icon. Like the play controls in the Videos app, these controls fade a few seconds after they first appear. To force them to reappear, just tap the display.

In addition to the play controls, you'll see a Favorite icon to the left of the play controls and a Share icon to the right (**Figure 8.13**). Tap Favorite, and the currently playing video is added to your YouTube favorites. Tap Share, and you see the expected sharing options that I describe in the "Featured" section earlier in this chapter.

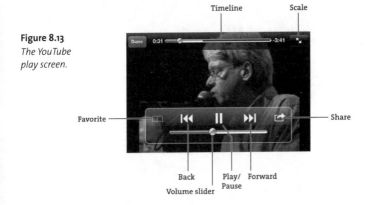

Figure 8.13
The YouTube play screen.

The video begins playing when the iPhone or iPod touch determines that it has downloaded enough data for the video to play from beginning to end without pausing to download more. When the video concludes, you'll see its More Info screen.

9

The Other Apps

I've covered the major areas of the iPhone and iPod touch: Siri, Phone, Mail, Safari, Music, Videos, Messages, Reminders, FaceTime, Photos, Calendar, YouTube, and the stores. It's time to turn to the smaller apps, which by default occupy the bulk of the Home screen on these devices: Maps, Weather, Notes, Clock, Game Center, Newsstand, Stocks, and the Utilities folder (which contains Calculator, Compass, and Voice Memos).

If you've used Mac OS X, many of these apps are familiar to you, as most of them are offered in that operating system as *widgets*—small applications that perform limited tasks. On the iPhone and iPod touch, they're considered to be full-blown apps, even though they're largely single-purpose programs. They work this way.

Maps

This app is a version of Google Maps made for iOS devices, and I've found it to be one of the iPhone's and iPod touch's most useful tools. It's not terribly useful, though, if you don't have a connection to the Internet—Wi-Fi or 3G on an iPhone and Wi-Fi on an iPod touch.

When you *are* connected to the Internet, you can use Maps to search for interesting locations (including businesses, residences, parks, and landmarks) near where you are or anywhere else in the world. It's the showcase app for these devices' Location Services feature. You can use it to get driving, walking, and public-transportation directions between here and there, and in some cases, you can check traffic conditions along your route.

The Maps app has two major components: Search and Directions. Each is available from the main Maps screen.

How Does Maps Know Where You Are?

You understand that Maps can pinpoint your location, but how? An iPhone uses three different technologies: GPS circuitry, which is built into the phone, and Wi-Fi and cell-tower triangulation. When you're outdoors, the iPhone uses its GPS capabilities to peer into the sky to connect to a satellite, which sends back your coordinates. Additionally, the iPhone scans for nearby Wi-Fi routers and cell-phone towers. It calculates the distance between these routers and towers to determine where you are (which is how your iPhone can judge its location when you're indoors and it can't "see" the sky).

(Continues on next page)

How Does Maps Know Where You Are? (continued)

An iPod touch lacks GPS circuitry, as well as the ability to communicate with cell towers. It relies solely on Wi-Fi triangulation, which is quite good when you're in an area that has a lot of these routers, but it does you little good when you've screaming down the local freeway. In such cases, your iPod touch is likely to be clueless about your location. For this reason, if you're considering using your iOS device as a portable GPS unit, the iPhone is the better item to have.

To find your location quickly, simply tap the small Location icon in the bottom-left corner of the Maps display. A blue dot appears on the map, indicating where the iPhone or iPod touch is. On an iPhone, you can tap this Location icon again, and the phone attempts to determine the direction in which you're facing, using the onboard compass. I find that knowing the direction in which I'm looking is helpful for navigating streets in an unfamiliar city.

Searching and exploring

If you have an iPhone 4S, one of the easiest ways to produce a map of a location you seek is to hold down the Home button and say to Siri, "Show me 555 Main Street, Anytown, USA." (You'll want, of course, to use a real address, in a real town, in a real state, province, or municipality.) Siri will respond by showing you a map of the location. Tap that map, and the Maps app opens, displaying that location. If you want to see directions to the location, don't tap the map; instead, tap Siri's microphone icon and ask, "How do I get there?" Siri opens the Maps app, where you'll see your route marked with a blue line.

Likewise, if you're already within the Maps app, just tap the Search field and then tap the Microphone button on the iPhone 4S's keyboard. Dictate the location and tap Done, and Maps should show you that location.

If you don't have an iPhone 4S or prefer to do things the old-fashioned way, you have another option. Launch Maps, and at the top of the screen, you see a Search field. Tap it, and up pops the keyboard. With that keyboard, you can enter any of a variety of search queries (**Figure 9.1**), including contacts (*Joe Blow*), a business name (*Apple, Inc.*), a town name (*Springfield*), a more-specific town name (*Springfield, MO*), a street or highway name (*Route 66*), a specific street name in a particular town (*Broadway, Springfield, MO*), or a thing (*Beer*).

Figure 9.1
*Maps' search
feature and the
results in the map
below.*

Tap for Google Street View.

Tap for Info screen.

Dog-ear icon

You can help Maps find its way by entering a more specific search, such as **Main St., Springfield, MO 65802** or **Beer 95521**. In short, the more specific you are in your query, the more accurate Maps will be.

Search views

You can display Maps' search results in four views:

- **Map**, which is a graphical illustration of the area

- **Satellite**, which is a photo captured by an orbiting satellite

- **Hybrid**, which is a satellite view with the names of roads overlaid

- **List**, which is a...well, *list* of all the locations pinpointed on the current map

These options are available when you tap the dog-eared-page icon in the bottom-right corner of the Maps screen (refer to Figure 9.1 in the preceding section). I cover the other options in this screen shortly.

In Map, Satellite, and Hybrid views, search results are denoted by red pushpins that drop onto the map. Tap one of these pins, and the name of the item appears in a description marker. Again, this name can be the name of a contact's address, business, town, or highway.

On the left side of many of these description markers is a round orange icon with a figure of a person inside. Tap this icon, and you see a Google Street View of the location—a series of 360-degree photographs of the area presented in landscape orientation. You can drag your finger around to "look" around. To move up or down the street, tap the arrow that overlays the street (**Figure 9.2**). To return to an overhead view, tap the map in the bottom-right corner of the screen.

Figure 9.2
Google Street View.

Map inset

The right side of the description marker bears a blue > icon. Tap this icon to go to the location's Info screen, which I cover in the next section.

Info screens

Info screens present any useful information that Maps can obtain about an item, including phone number, email, address, and home-page URL (**Figure 9.3**). The email and URL links are *live*, meaning that when you tap an email address, Mail opens and addresses a message to that contact, and when you tap a URL, Safari opens and displays that Web site.

Figure 9.3
A Maps Info screen.

At the bottom of each Info screen, you'll see five labeled buttons: Directions To Here, Directions From Here, Add to Contacts, Share Location, and Add to Bookmarks. (You may have to scroll the screen to see all these buttons.) They work this way:

- **Directions To Here.** Tap this button to display Maps' Driving Directions interface (which I explain shortly), with the item's address in the End field.

- **Directions From Here.** This feature works similarly. The difference is that the item's address appears in the Driving Directions Start field.

- **Add to Contacts.** This button produces a sheet that bears three new buttons: Create New Contact, Add to Existing Contact, and Cancel. Tap the first button, and a New Contact screen appears with the information from the Info screen filled in. You're welcome to add any other information you like, using the standard contact-field tools.

  As for the Add to Existing Contact button, say that your buddy Brabanzio has just started putting in his 8 hours at the local pickle works. You can use Maps to locate said works, tap this icon, and add its information to his contact information.

- **Share Location.** If you've found the perfect sushi joint and want to tell your friends, tap this button. A sheet appears, offering you the choice to share via email, message, or tweet. Tap Email, and an unaddressed email message pops up. The message's Subject heading includes the name of the location, and the message body contains a link that, when clicked by a recipient, launches a browser and opens Google Maps to that location. Tap Message, and the Messages app opens, with a link to the location embedded in a new message. Tap Tweet, and a new Twitter message appears, with the location embedded as a URL.

- **Add to Bookmarks.** You can bookmark locations in Maps. Tapping this icon brings up the Add Bookmark screen, where you can rename the bookmark, if you like. When you're done, tap Save, and that location is available in Maps' Bookmarks screen (which, again, I get to shortly).

Bookmarks

The Search field includes a very helpful Bookmarks button. Tap this button to bring up a list of all the locations you've bookmarked, as well as recent search terms and your list of contacts (**Figure 9.4**).

Figure 9.4
Maps' Bookmarks screen.

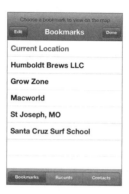

To remove, rename, or reorder select bookmarks, tap the Edit button. In the resulting screen, you can tap the now-expected red minus (–) icon to produce the Delete icon, which you tap to remove the bookmark. You can also tap the bookmark to show the Edit Bookmark screen, where you can edit the bookmark's name. Finally, you can reorder bookmarks by dragging them up or down in the list.

Recents

Tap the Recents button at the bottom of the Bookmarks screen, and you'll see a list of the previous 20 searches done on your iPhone or iPod touch. As you conduct a new search, the last search in this list is deleted. These queries are categorized by Search (*pizza*), Start and End (*home to Bob's house*), Location (*Grand Rapids*), and Contact (*Ebenezer Scrooge*). Tap one of these entries, and you see its location—or, in the case of driving directions, locations—on the map.

Contacts

It's swell that your Aunt Vilma sent you a change-of-address card, but where the heck is Fort Dodge, Iowa? Tap the Contacts button at the

bottom of the Bookmarks screen, find Aunt Vilma's name in the long list
of contacts, tap her name, and then tap the street address of her new
cabin down by the river. Maps will pin her palace in next to no time.

Other dog-eared-page options

In addition to having access to Map, Satellite, Hybrid, and List views when
you tap the dog-ear icon, you have the three options shown in **Figure 9.5**:

Figure 9.5
*The dog-ear
screen.*

- **Drop Pin.** The first option allows you to drop your own pin on the map.
  Tap Drop Pin; the dog-ear page flips down, and a purple pin appears
  on the map currently displayed onscreen. You can drag the pin where
  you want it. The address of whatever's under the pin appears below
  the words *Dropped Pin*. Tap the > icon, and you're taken to the dropped
  pin's Info screen. In addition to the options offered in a regular Info
  screen, this screen includes a Remove Pin button for doing just that.

> **tip** Why would you want to bookmark a movable pin? I often do this
> when I'm out and about and need to enter a couple of temporary
> locations. I may drop a pin, tap the blue icon, tap the Add to Bookmarks button,
> and then call the pin Where I Parked the Car. Then I'm at liberty to drop another
> pin during that same journey to mark a different important stop. Later, when I
> need to retrieve my car, I can call up the appropriate bookmark.

- **Print.** If you have a supported printer connected to your network (I discuss printing in Chapter 10), you can print out a map of a marked location. The map contains the image of the location, at exactly the zoom level you've used on the device, along with the name of the location and its address.

- **Show Traffic.** If the area you're viewing in Maps supports the Traffic feature (not all areas do), tap the Show Traffic button to see colored lines that indicate how congested the roads are. Green denotes good traffic flow, yellow is somewhat congested, and red is stop-and-go traffic (or sometimes just stop). Yellow and red areas on the map throb so that they're more noticeable. If the service isn't supported in the area you're looking at, the Info screen reads *Traffic Unavailable in This Area*.

tip Be sure to zoom in on the map when you see yellow and red traffic warnings. The warning may apply to only one direction of traffic—with luck, the direction you're *not* traveling in. A zoomed-in view will tell you what you're up against.

Getting directions

Maps' Directions component is useful too. Feed it the locations where you'd like to start and where you'd like to end up, and it provides a reasonable route for getting there, like so:

1. Tap Directions at the bottom of the Maps screen.

   Empty Start and End fields appear at the top of the screen.

2. Tap the Start field.

   If you've used the Location Services feature to tell it where you are (see the sidebar "How Does Maps Know Where You Are?" earlier in this chapter), the Start field automatically displays *Current Location* in blue letters. You're welcome to use that location as the start point. If you prefer to use a different start point, simply tap the field again and then tap the X icon at the right end of the field to clear it.

3. Using the keyboard (or your voice in league with the iPhone 4S's dictation feature), enter the location where you want to begin your journey.

This location can be something as generic as a zip code or as specific as your home address. Alternatively, you can tap the Bookmarks icon and then tap a bookmark in the resulting screen; its location will appear in the Start field.

4. Tap the End field.

Same idea—type or dictate a location, or choose a bookmark (**Figure 9.6**).

Figure 9.6
Entering start and end points for driving directions.

5. Tap the blue Route button in the top-right corner.

Maps presents an overview map that may contain more than one route. The first route is the one your iPhone or iPod touch recommends; the others are alternatives. Just above the map, you see the amount of time Maps believes it will take you to reach your destination, along with the number of miles from start to finish. Tap a different route; that route appears in dark blue, and the information pane above the map changes to reflect the time and distance of the new selected route.

At the top of the screen are three transportation icons representing driving, public transportation, and walking routes. Each icon, when selected, displays the length of the journey and how long it should take—*39 minutes - 30.06 miles* if you've chosen the driving option, for example (**Figure 9.7**).

Figure 9.7
Trip overview.

The Public Transportation icon is likely to display different information from the Driving icon. It tells you when the next mode of transportation (which could be a bus, subway, or train, or a combination) is going to leave and when it's likely to arrive.

Tap the Walking button, and you see the most reasonable route you can take on foot (meaning no freeways), the distance, and the time it should take to get where you're going. (The walking estimates are unreasonable for long distances. Maps told me that I could walk 200 miles in less than three days, for example. Uh, no.)

The Map, Satellite, and Hybrid buttons on the dog-ear page do exactly what you'd expect, but the List button's functionality changes when you're using the Directions feature.

Tap List, and the twists and turns of your route are laid out in numbered steps—say, 1 *Drive 0.4 miles then turn right at Old Codger Road.* 2 *Drive 2.6 miles then merge onto CA-94 W toward Tokyo.* Tap a step, and Maps displays that portion of your trip on a map, circling the important twist or turn outlined in the step, as well as displaying the written driving directions for that step at the top of the screen.

To view the next turn in your trip, just tap the right-arrow icon at the top of the screen. To return to the map overview of your trip, tap the dog-ear icon; tap List; and then tap the Route Overview entry at the top of the Directions screen.

> **tip** When you return to List view, a purple circle surrounds the step in the list that corresponds to the portion of the trip you just viewed. If the fourth part of the trip was to turn left on Dankhippie Road, for example, a purple circle appears around the number 4.

If you like this turn-by-turn graphic overview of your route, you can skip the List icon. Just tap the Start button in the top-right corner of the route overview screen. The first step of your journey will be shown in all its graphic glory, along with the accompanying text at the top of the screen. Tap the right-arrow icon to proceed to the next step (**Figure 9.8**). Should you want to edit your route—change the start or end point—just tap the Edit button in the top-left corner of the display. The Start and End fields appear, along with the keyboard.

Figure 9.8
Viewing a trip.

At this point, you can return to your journey by tapping the Cancel button in the top-right corner or plot a new journey by tapping Clear.

Weather

Weather is another app that owes more than a tip of the hat to a Mac OS X widget. Though the layout of the Weather app is vertical rather than horizontal, it contains the same information as its namesake widget: a six-day forecast (including the current day); current temperature in Fahrenheit or Celsius (selectable from the app's information screen); each day's projected highs and lows; and icons that represent the current or projected weather conditions, such as sun, clouds, snow, or rain. Tap the display, and you see today's hourly forecast (**Figure 9.9**); tap again to return to the daily view.

Figure 9.9
An hourly forecast within the Weather app.

To move from one location screen to the next, simply swipe your finger horizontally across the screen. Alternatively, just tap to the right or left of the small white dots that appear at the bottom of the screen. (These dots indicate how many locations you have saved.)

Tap the *i* icon in the bottom-right corner of the Weather screen, and the screen flips around to display all the locations you've saved. If you'd like the local weather to appear in the number-one position in the app, ensure that the Local Weather switch is set to On. Now, wherever you are, the app will display the local conditions and forecast, based on the iPhone's or iPod touch's location information.

To add a new location, tap the plus (+) icon; use the keyboard to enter a location (again, a zip code is a handy shortcut); and tap Search. To remove a location, tap it; tap the red minus icon; and then tap Delete. To switch from Fahrenheit to Celsius, tap the appropriate icon at the bottom of the screen. To reorder locations, just drag them up or down in the list.

> **tip** Weather is another app in which Siri shines. If you have an iPhone 4S, just invoke Siri and command, "What's the weather like?" Siri will present a six-day forecast for wherever you are at the moment. You can also ask for weather in other locations ("What's the weather like in Alice Springs?").

Notes

Notes is the iPhone's and iPod touch's simple text editor—and by *simple*, I mean downright rudimentary. Tap Notes in the Home screen and then tap the plus icon in the top-right corner of the resulting screen to create a new note. When you do, the familiar keyboard appears. Start typing your new novel (OK, novelette). If you make a mistake, use the usual text-editing tricks to repair your work. If you have an iPhone 4S, ou needn't type. Just tap the keyboard's Microphone button and start talking. Remember to speak punctuation too ("I love your hair period could I borrow it question mark").

Each individual Notes screen has four icons at the bottom. The left-arrow and right-arrow icons do exactly what you'd expect: move to the previous or next note. Tap the Send icon, and Notes presents two choices: Email and Print. Tap Email and a new, unaddressed email message opens in Mail, with the note's text appearing in the message body. Tap Print, and the note prints on a compatible printer on your local network. Tap the Trash icon, and you'll be offered the option to Delete Note or Cancel.

To view a list of all your notes (**Figure 9.10**), tap the Notes icon in the top-left corner of the screen. Each note is titled with up to the first 30 characters of the note. (If you entered a return character after the first line, only the text in that first line appears as the note's title.) Next to each note is the date of its creation (or time, if it was created that day). Time and date information also appears at the top of each note.

Figure 9.10
Notes app.

Clock

More than just a simple timepiece, the Clock app includes four components—World Clock, Alarm, Stopwatch, and Timer—that are available as icons arrayed across the bottom of the app's screen. Here's what they do.

World Clock

Just as its name implies, World Clock allows you to track time in multiple locations. Clocks are presented in both analog and digital form

(**Figure 9.11**). On analog clocks, day is indicated by a white clock and night by a black one.

Figure 9.11
World Clock.

To add a new clock to the list, just tap the plus icon in the top-right corner of the screen. In the Search field of the resulting screen, enter the name of a reasonably significant city or a country. The device includes a database of such locations and offers suggestions as you type.

You can remove or reorder these clocks. To delete a clock, tap the Edit button and then tap the clock's red minus icon. To reposition a clock, tap its right side and then drag it up or down in the list.

Alarm

Your iPhone or iPod touch can get you out of bed in the morning or remind you of important events. Just tap Alarm at the bottom of the screen and then tap the plus icon to add an alarm.

In the Add Alarm screen, you'll find a Repeat entry, which lets you order an alarm to repeat each week on a particular day; a Sound entry, where you assign one of the device's 25 ringtones to your alarm (tap Buy More

Tones to be taken to the iTunes Store, where you can purchase additional ringtones); an On/Off Snooze entry, which tells the device to give you 10 more minutes of shuteye when you click the Home button; and a Label entry that lets you assign a message to an alarm (*Get Up, Meeting This Morning,* or *Take That Big Purple Pill,* for example).

To create a new alarm, just flick the hour, minute, and AM/PM wheels to set a time for the alarm; then tap Save. When you save at least one alarm and switch that alarm on, a small clock icon appears in the iPhone's or iPod touch's status bar.

tip You can create an alarm only for the current 24-hour period. If you'd like an alarm to go off at a time later than that, use the Calendar app to create a new event and then attach an alert to that event, or use the Reminders app to create a reminder for a specific day.

Stopwatch

The iPhone's and iPod touch's Stopwatch app includes a timer that displays hours, seconds, and tenths of seconds. Tap Start, and the timer begins to run. Tap Stop, and the timer pauses. Tap Start again, and the timer takes up where it left off. Tap Reset, and the timer resets to 00:00.0.

While the timer runs, you can tap the Lap button, and a lap time will be recorded in the list below. Subsequent taps of Lap add more lap times to the list. When you tap Lap, the counter resets to 0.

Timer

The Clock app also offers a timer that can tick down from as little as 1 minute to as much as 23 hours and 59 minutes. To work the timer, just use the hour and minute wheels to select the amount of time you'd like the timer to run; then tap Start. (Alternatively, you can tap a number on the wheel, and the wheel advances to the "go" position.) The timer displays a countdown in hours, minutes, and seconds, and the Start button changes to Cancel. Tap this Cancel button to stop the countdown.

The device performs one of two actions when the timer ends: It plays one of its ringtones and displays a Timer Done dialog box, or it activates the Sleep iPod feature (yes, it's called that on the iPhone too). The latter option isn't as odd as it first sounds. Many people like to listen to soothing music or ambient sounds as they drift off to sleep. The Sleep iPod option allows them to do just that without playing the device all night and needlessly running down the battery.

Game Center

Game Center is Apple's social-gaming network. With Game Center, you can add friends, invite those friends (or strangers) to play multiplayer games with you, earn achievements in your favorite games, and check the rankings of particular games' best players. Game Center is intuitive enough that I'll largely leave it to you to explore. Simply make sure that you have an Apple ID, enter your password, and move to the Friends screen to add friends you want to play with.

Newsstand

Newsstand is a place where you can access newspapers and electronic magazines. In a strict sense, it's not really an app like the others on the Home screen. Rather, it's more like an intelligent folder. Tap it, and you see an empty shelf that bears a Store button. Tap the Store button, and you're taken to the Newsstand section of the App Store, where some newspaper and magazine apps are offered. To download one—and subsequently have it appear within Newsstand—just tap the purchase button as you would with any other app.

If that app is compatible with Newsstand, it appears not on the Home screen when it downloads, but within Newsstand (**Figure 9.12**). When you tap the publication's icon within Newsstand, the app launches and displays the app's content.

Figure 9.12
Viewing the contents of Newsstand.

note Many apps that appear in Newsstand aren't full publications. Rather, they're simply vehicles for purchasing a subscription to the papers or magazines in question.

Stocks

The Stocks app has a lot in common with the Mac OS X Stocks widget. Like that widget, the app displays your chosen stocks and market indexes (Dow Jones Industrial Average and NASDAQ, for example) in the top part of the screen and performance statistics below. Next to each index or stock-ticker symbol, you'll see the almost-current share price (results are delayed by 20 minutes), such as *AAPL 392.87*, followed by the day's gain or loss as represented by a green (gain) or red (loss) icon.

By default, the app represents gains and losses in points—such as −2.44. To see the company's market cap—365.1B, for example—tap one of these red or green icons. You can toggle to a percentage view by tapping an icon again. Tap once more to return to point view.

note Your iPhone or iPod touch must be connected to the Internet for the results to appear.

To view statistics for a particular index or stock, just tap its name. A graph at the bottom of the screen charts that index's or stock's performance over 1 day, 1 week, 1 month, 3 months, 6 months, 1 year, or 2 years. To choose a time period, just tap the appropriate icon (such as 1d for 1 day or 6m for 6 months).

If you flip the device to landscape orientation, you see this graph enlarged. No, this feature isn't for the benefit of people with poor eyesight. Tap and hold this graph, and an orange line appears that tells you the stock price at the time. (The date appears at the top of the screen.) Tap with two fingers, and the iPhone or iPod touch tells you the change in points and percentage between one finger and another. So, for example, you might select Apple's stock in 6-month view; place your left index finger on May 31, 2011; and put your right index finger on October 20, 2011 (**Figure 9.13**). You see that the stock rose 47.36 points, or 13.71 percent.

Figure 9.13
Stocks app.

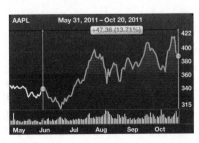

Return the device to portrait orientation and swipe a graph to the left, and you'll see news headlines related to the company. (This window scrolls down if there are enough headlines to merit scrolling.) Tap a headline, and Safari launches and displays the story. Swipe once more to the left, and you'll see a table of statistics related to the company, including such details as the day's opening and closing prices and trading volume.

If you tap the *i* (Information) icon in the bottom-right corner of the display, the screen flips to reveal the indexes and stocks that appear on the app's front page. Click the plus icon in the top-left corner and use the keyboard to add a ticker symbol or company name. In the case of a company name, the device will search for matches. If you type **Apple** and tap Search, for example, you'll get a list that includes not only Apple, Inc., but also Appleton Group Plus and Appleseed Institutional. Tap the search result you want, and it will be added to the bottom of the list. You can reorder the list by dragging an entry up or down in the list by its reorder bar to the right of the entry. To remove items, just tap the red minus icon next to the item's name and then tap the resulting Delete icon.

The Information screen also includes three icons: %, Price, and Mkt Cap. Tap one to determine the default display of gains and losses in the main Stocks screen. This screen also offers an obvious icon. To have Safari take you to the Yahoo Finance page, simply tap Yahoo! Finance at the bottom of the screen.

Calculator

Unless you've stubbornly clung to your grandfather's abacus, you've used an electronic calculator like this before. Similar to the dime-a-dozen calculators you can find on your computer or at the local Bean Counters "R" Us, the Calculator app performs addition, subtraction, division, and multiplication operations up to nine places when you hold the device in portrait orientation. When you choose an operation (addition or subtraction, for example), Calculator highlights the appropriate symbol by circling it.

In addition to the 0–9 digits and the divide, multiply, add, subtract, and equal keys, you find these keys:

- **mc** (for *memory clear*). This key clears out any number stored in the calculator's memory.

- **m+.** Tap m+ to add the displayed number to the number in memory. If no number is in memory, tapping m+ stores the displayed number in memory.

- **m–.** Tap m– to subtract the displayed number from the memorized number.

- **mr.** Tap mr, and the displayed number replaces the currently memorized number. A white ring appears around this key if a number is in memory.

- **C.** Tap C to clear the total.

Ah, but wait—there's more. Flip the iPhone or iPod touch to landscape orientation, and you get a full-featured scientific calculator (**Figure 9.14**). When you rotate the device, any number stored in the calculator remains, so you can move quickly from simple to complex calculations and back again without losing your work.

Figure 9.14
The Calculator app's scientific calculator.

Compass (iPhone Only)

The iPhone 3GS, iPhone 4, and iPhone 4S have a built-in magnetometer—a bit of circuitry that measures the direction of the Earth's magnetic field. Launch this app, and the iPhone is likely to tell you the direction it's pointing in by using a traditional compass face.

At the bottom of the screen are the geographic coordinates (degrees, minutes, and seconds indicating where the iPhone believes that it is). Tap these coordinates, and the iPhone may display an address to accompany your location. To the left of these coordinates is the Location icon. Tap it, and Maps opens, showing you your location as determined by the iPhone. In the bottom-right corner of the Compass screen is the Info button. Tap it, and you can choose whether the iPhone points to true north or magnetic north.

 Compass doesn't work unless you have Location Services turned on.

Voice Memos

Voice Memos is—unsurprisingly, given its name—an app for recording audio. That audio can be recorded with the iPhone's or iPod touch's built-in microphone or with the microphone on a headset plugged into the device's Headphone port. To record and play back a memo, follow these steps:

1. Launch Voice Memos, and start talking—but don't record yet.

   Keep an eye on the VU meter at the bottom of the screen. If you see the needle move, the iPhone or iPod touch can "hear" you. This needle isn't very accurate, though, so don't try to push it up near the red. If it gets anywhere near the –10 mark, you're loud enough.

2. Tap the red Record icon in the bottom-left corner of the screen, and start talking for real.

A red bar appears at the top of the screen, indicating that the device is recording (**Figure 9.15**).

Figure 9.15
Voice Memos app at work.

3. Pause, if you like, by tapping Record again.

To resume, tap Record one more time.

4. Stop recording.

Tap the silver button to the right of the VU meter, and your recording is saved.

5. Tap the List button in the bottom-right corner of the screen to play your memo.

A Voice Memos screen appears, listing all the voice memos you've recorded. To play one, just tap it (and tap it again to pause). The timeline at the bottom of the screen displays the progress of the playback. You can tap and drag the playhead to move forward or backward in the memo.

6. Trim it.

   Tap the blue > icon next to a voice memo to display the memo's Info screen; then tap the Trim Memo button. When you do, a pane appears that includes a yellow trim bar. Drag the ends of the trim bar to cut off the beginning and/or end of the memo. You can hear what's left by tapping the Play button next to the bar.

   To throw out the stuff you've trimmed, tap Trim Voice Memo. (This action is permanent, so be careful.)

   This Info window also contains a Share button, which saves you the trouble of backing up a screen if you want to email or message the memo to someone.

7. Share it.

   A memo's Info screen also include a Share button. Tap it, and a pane floats up with Email, Message, and Cancel buttons in it. Tap Email, and up pops an unaddressed email message containing the memo as an attachment. Tap Message, and Messages opens with the audio file attached to a message.

8. Label it.

   Tap the name of your memo—*5:15 PM 00:17*, for example—in the Info window, and a Label screen comes into view. Tap the label that best categorizes your memo—such as Podcast, Lecture, or Idea—and your memo is labeled accordingly. (You can also enter a custom label by tapping Custom at the bottom of the screen and typing a label name in the succeeding screen.) That label name replaces the time/date name in the Voice Memos screen.

When you sync your device to your computer, the voice memos you've recorded are transferred to your iTunes Library. Regrettably, the label names you've applied don't transfer as well. These memos retain their date-and-time titles.

10

Tips and Troubleshooting

The iPhone and iPod touch are dreams of intuitive design and ease of use. Yet nothing in this world (save you, dear reader, and I) is completely foolproof or infallible, which is why this chapter is necessary.

Within these pages, I offer ways to get things done more expeditiously, provide hints for operating these devices in ways that may not seem obvious, and (of course) tell you what to do when your iPhone or iPod touch does the Bad Thing and stops behaving as it should.

Getting Tipsy

I've sprinkled tips and hints throughout the book, but I saved a few good ones for this chapter. In the following sections, I show you how to control text, manage the battery, and sync your iPhone or iPod touch efficiently, as well as find the device if it goes missing.

The word on text

If one iOS feature frustrates the greatest number of people from the get-go, it's text entry. These tips will help make you a better iPhone and iPod typist.

Dictate if you can

If you have an iPhone 4S, take advantage of its dictation capabilities. Yes, it will seem clumsy talking to your phone, mouthing words like *"Dear Mary comma new paragraph please pick up the froggy jammies hyphen you know the ones I mean hyphen that I ordered last week period new paragraph thanks very much comma John",* but if you speak clearly and in an orderly way, you'll find text entry much easier.

Keep going

Typing on the keyboard isn't like typing on your computer keyboard, a process in which you type, make a mistake, backspace to correct the mistake, and continue typing. Use that technique on the iPhone or iPod touch, and you'll go nuts making all the corrections.

Typing the first letter correctly is important, as mistyping that first letter is likely to send the device's predictive powers in the wrong direction. But after that, get as close as you can to the correct letters and continue typing even if you make a mistake. More often than not, the device's predictive-typing feature will correct the mistake for you (**Figure 10.1**). To take the suggestion, tap the spacebar; the iPhone or iPod touch will fill in the (ideally) correct word.

Figure 10.1
Often, your iPhone or iPod touch knows what you meant to type.

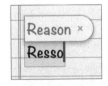

Sure, you may need to go back and correct a word or two in a couple of sentences by pressing and holding the display to bring up the magnifying-glass icon, but doing this for two mistakes is far more efficient than retyping half a dozen words.

Move to the correct letter

You need to type as carefully as possible in one specific instance: when you're entering a password. As I mention elsewhere, for security reasons, the iPhone and iPod touch very briefly display the last letter you typed in a password field before turning that letter into a black dot. This brevity makes it nigh-on impossible to correct your work because you can't see where you've made a mistake.

For this reason, when you're entering passwords (or just typing carefully), tap a character, and wait for the letter to pop up on the display. If you've hit the wrong character, keep your finger on the display, and move it to the correct character. Only when you release your finger will the device accept the character.

tip   This "doesn't count until you let go" technique also applies to the Camera button in the Camera app. Tap and hold the button while you frame your shot. Let go of it when you're ready to take the picture.

Adjust the dictionary

Are you irked because the iPhone or iPod touch invariably suggests *candles* when you intended to type *dandles* (**Figure 10.2**)? You have the power to modify the device's built-in dictionary. If you begin to type *dandles*, but the iPhone or iPod touch displays *candles*, simply tap the suggestion, and it disappears. Then finish typing.

Figure 10.2
Correct the dictionary by tapping incorrect suggestions.

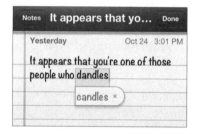

In the future, the device shouldn't suggest *candles*, *dandies*, or *dangles* but should let you type *dandles* without butting in—though it may have more creative choices up its sleeve, as *dandles* is an uncommonly used word. Regrettably, it's unlikely to add *dandles* to its list of suggestions and offer it after you've typed *dand,* as the iPhone and iPod touch can be stubborn about adding new autocomplete words.

Avoid unnecessary capitalizations and contractions

The iPhone and iPod touch try to make as much sense as possible from your typing. When they're willing to, let them carry the load. You probably won't type the letter *i* all by itself unless you mean *I*, for example. The iPhone and iPod touch know this and will make a lone *i* a capital *I*. Similarly, type *ill*, and even if you're trying to say that you're not feeling well, the device will suggest *I'll*. Conversely, if you're feeling fine, the iPhone or iPod touch allows you to type *well* without suggesting *we'll*. You need to be careful about *its* and *it's*, however. These devices always suggest *it's*, which could drive the nitpicking grammarians in your life to distraction.

Rule of thumb: When a word that can also be spelled as a contraction is tossed at the iPhone or iPod touch, it almost always suggests the more commonly used word (**Figure 10.3**).

Figure 10.3
You can often skip the apostrophes when typing on the iPhone or iPod touch.

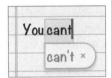

Space out your periods

No, I don't mean place spaces between them. I mean when you reach the end of a sentence, don't bother going to the .?123 keyboard to enter a period. Just tap the spacebar twice in succession. The device will end the last word you typed with a period, insert a space, and configure the Shift key so that the next letter you type will be capitalized. Now you're ready to type the next sentence.

 note You can turn off this double-tap spacebar behavior by switching the setting off in the Keyboard portion of the General setting.

Power management

Wonderful as it is to have an iPhone or iPod touch that can play full-length movies, you do *not* want to board a cross-country flight, enjoy the latest Harry Potter flick on your device, jump off the plane with the expectation of calling or texting home for a long "I arrived safely" chat, and be greeted by a dead battery. Power can be paramount in such situations. To help ensure that your battery will still have something to offer, try these tips.

Treat it right

Your iPhone's or iPod touch's battery performs its best in these conditions:

- **It's warm.** The battery performs best when it's run at around room temperature. If it gets cold—below 24°F—it doesn't hold a charge as long.

- **But not too warm.** Running a cool iPhone or iPod touch won't damage the battery, but storing it somewhere that's really hot—say, your car's glove compartment when it's 95°F outside—can.

Lock it

The iPhone and iPod touch aren't supposed to do anything unless you touch their display or click the Home button, but you might accidentally do one thing or the other if the device is rattling around loose in your pocket or pocketbook. Rather than project all 216 minutes of *Lawrence of Arabia* to the inside of your pants pocket, quickly press the Sleep/Wake button to lock your device.

Turn off Sound Check and EQ

The iPhone's and iPod touch's music features—Sound Check and EQ (equalizer)—require more processing power from your device, in turn pulling more power from your battery. If you've applied EQ settings in iTunes to the tracks that will play on your device, you must set the iPhone's or iPod touch's EQ setting to Flat rather than Off, which essentially tells the device to ignore any EQ settings imposed by iTunes. To make EQ Flat, choose Settings > Music > EQ, and tap Flat in the EQ screen.

Turn off syncing

When iCloud reaches out to sync mail, contacts, calendars, reminders, bookmarks, and notes, or pushes photos around with Photo Stream, more

is demanded of your iPhone's or iPod touch's processor, which drains
the battery. Syncing in the background is great, but if it leaves you with
a drained battery too often, turn it off by tapping Settings > iCloud and
flipping the On switches to Off.

Turn off Siri (iPhone 4S)

Siri works its magic by connecting to the Internet—which also draws
power from the battery. If you use Siri a lot, it drains your battery quickly.
If you can't resist Siri's charms, leave it on, but use it sparingly. Otherwise,
switch it off by tapping Settings > General > Siri.

Turn off Wi-Fi

Turning off Wi-Fi can help you get more life from your battery charge.
To turn off Wi-Fi, go to the Settings screen, tap Wi-Fi, and flip the toggle
switch to Off.

Turn off Bluetooth

Yes, Bluetooth can stress a battery too. Turn it off by going to the General
setting, tapping Bluetooth, and flicking the switch in the resulting
Bluetooth screen to Off.

Turn off Location Services

This option is another one that can drain a battery, as the iPhone or
iPod touch looks around every so often to see where it is. You can turn
Location Services off by tapping Settings > Location Services.

Fetch mail less often

Push mail and accounts configured to fetch messages automatically
every 15 minutes tax your battery's charge. If you don't need your mail

Right Now, turn push mail off and configure mail fetching so that it's done manually (when you launch the Mail app). You do this in the Fetch New Data screen within the Mail, Contacts, Calendars setting.

Troubleshooting Power Problems

If you notice that your device is sucking down the battery like a tourist chugging Mai Tais on a Hawaiian sunset cruise, there are ways to zero in on what's causing the problem:

1. Tap Settings > General > About > Diagnostics & Usage.

2. Tap the Diagnostics & Usage Data button.

   You're taken to a Data screen, which reports things that have gone wrong with your device.

3. If you see a CrashReport entry, tap it, and try to learn from it what the problem may be.

   Among all the gibberish, you may see mention of contacts or calendar events that are part of the problem. In such cases, you want to remove the suspect items from your device and then resync in the hope that a new copy cures the problem.

Having a tool such as Recession Apps' System Activity Monitor (available for 99 cents at the App Store) can be useful. It shows you the device's running processes, along with a constantly updating graph of processor use. If you regularly see readings in the 40 percent–to–60 percent range, something is wrong with your iPhone or iPod touch. Also, if you see CrashReport entries cropping up every so often, your device could be in a crashing loop, which will chew up your battery charge. Again, take a look at the Diagnostic & Usage Data reports in the hope of ferreting out the bad guy.

Plug it in

If you're accustomed to the way that traditional iPods work, you may be under the impression that when you jack your iPhone or iPod touch into your computer's USB port, you can't use it. Wrong. When it's plugged into its power supply, your computer, or an accessory device that supplies power, the device is completely usable. There's no need to unmount it to watch movies, surf the Net, or get email; everything works.

And now that you can sync your device wirelessly, there's no reason to plug it into your computer to charge or sync it. Turn on iTunes Wi-Fi Sync (within the General setting), jack it into a powered outlet, ensure that it's on the same network as your computer, and let the syncing begin.

Device gone missing

The iPhone and iPod touch are small enough and out of your pocket often enough that they're easy to misplace. Whether one of these things has slipped behind a couch cushion or you left it in the back of a cab, you'd like to know where it is. The Find My iPhone/iPod feature lets you do just that.

To use Find My iPhone/iPod, you must have an iCloud account, which is free. Also, before you can use this feature, you must switch it on (meaning that you have to do this *before* you lose your device). Just follow these steps:

1. Choose Settings > iCloud.

2. Enable Find My iPhone/iPod by flicking the On/Off switch to On.

3. Open your computer's Web browser, and travel to www.icloud.com, which is iCloud's log-in page.

4. Log in to iCloud by entering your user name and password.

   iCloud's Mail page opens by default.

5. If the Web page doesn't automatically open to the Find My iPhone page, click the icon of a cloud in the top-left corner.

note Yes, in iCloud this feature is called *Find My iPhone* (as it was first implemented on the iPhone), even though it's called *Find My iPod* on the iPod touch and *Find My iPad* on an iPad.

   A window appears, containing (among other things) a Find My iPhone button.

6. Click the Find My iPhone button, and verify your password.

7. Locate your device.

   In the page that appears, you see a world map with the words *Trying to Locate* at the top. Any iOS devices you own for which the "Find My" option has been enabled appear in a Devices list on the left side of the page. Eventually, the page updates, placing a green dot next to any devices that it's located. If your device is switched on, if it's connected to a Wi-Fi or 3G network, and if the Find My option is enabled on the iPhone or iPod touch, the device you're looking for should be among the devices found. Click the name of your device, and the map shows its location, pinpointed by a green dot.

tip Again, if the device isn't switched on and within range of a Wi-Fi or 3G network that provides location information, the Find My iPhone page won't work, and your device won't be located. Instead, you'll see a gray dot next to its name and the word *Offline* below it.

8. Communicate with the device.

Click your iPhone or iPod touch on the map, and its name appears on the map, along with an Info button.

9. Click the Info button.

This button reveals the Info window (**Figure 10.4**), where you see three options:

Figure 10.4
Find My iPhone has found my iPhone along California's scenic Highway 1.

- **Play Sound or Send Message.** If you know that you've left your iPhone or iPod touch in a place where someone may find it—a restaurant or a doctor's office, for example—click Play Sound or Send Message. Type something polite in the resulting message field, such as *Please return my iPhone by calling 555-555-1212. Thank you.* To help get the finder's attention, enable the Play Sound option, too. Then click Send. The message will appear on the device when it's next connected to a Wi-Fi or 3G network (**Figure 10.5**). If you've enabled the Sound option, a not-terribly-obnoxious alert sound plays at full volume for two minutes.

Figure 10.5
Let the device's finder know that you're on his trail.

tip The Play Sound option is also perfect for those times when you know that your iPhone or iPod touch is in your house somewhere, but you can't find it.

- **Remote Lock.** If you think there's some possibility that you'll get your iPhone or iPod touch back, click the Remote Lock button in the Info window, and enter a four-digit passcode to prevent the person who has the device from accessing its data. Later, when the device is back in your possession, you can unlock it with this passcode.

- **Remote Wipe.** If all else fails, and you're certain that the device is lost or in the wrong hands, you should wipe its data. To do that, click the Remote Wipe button in the Info window. This feature permanently deletes all the media and data on the device. Because it does, you're asked to confirm that you really want to do this and understand that you can't undo or stop this action. If you're sure, click Erase All Data.

If you wipe the iPhone or iPod touch remotely and later recover it, you can always restore its data and media by syncing it with your computer. Remember, iTunes keeps a backup when you sync.

note True to its slogan "There's an app for that," Apple has a Find My iPhone app that allows you to do all this from an iOS device. If you have an iPhone, an iPad, or an iPod touch, you can install this app and use it to locate your device (and then send it a message, lock it, or wipe its information).

Printing

If you truly embraced the iPhone and iPod touch as being small computers rather than just a cool phone and a cool media player, the idea that you couldn't print directly from these devices once drove you up the wall. With iOS 4.2, Apple introduced printing to iOS devices, including the two that are the subject of this book. It works this way.

The supported way

After the many "See Chapter 10 for the ins-and-outs of printing" references throughout these pages, I'm almost sorry to tell you how easy it is. These devices use a technology called AirPrint to communicate with compatible printers. For this technology to work the way it was designed to, you must have an AirPrint-compatible printer. HP has been the leading supporter of AirPrint among companies that make printers, but Epson and Canon also have printers that support it.

As long as you see *AirPrint* on the printer's box, pretty much all you need to do is switch on the printer and then follow these steps:

1. Make sure that the printer is using the same network as your iPhone or iPod touch.

2. Enable the printer's AirPrint feature, if it's not on by default.

    See the printer's manual for details.

3. Tap Print on your iOS device in any app that supports printing.

    A Printer Options screen appears, offering two options: Printer and 1 Copy.

4. Do one of the following:

   - To print a single copy of the document, tap Printer to see the available printers; then tap the one you want to use. You return to the Printer Options screen, which now bears a Print button.

   - To print more than one copy of the document, tap 1 Copy and then tap the plus button to set the number of copies.

5. Tap Print, and that's what happens.

The sneakier way

I can understand if, after reading the last few paragraphs, you sputtered, "Wait—I have to drop $100 or more for a new printer just to print from my iPhone or iPod touch?!?" No, you don't have to. There are other ways. Those other ways are a couple of applications that you run on your computer.

If you have a Mac, Ecamm Networks (http://ecamm.com) offers the $20 Printopia 2 for Mac. Install it on your Mac, and any printers attached to that Mac via a wired or network connection are available for you to print to from your iOS devices. Also, you can send documents directly to the Mac, Evernote (www.evernote.com), or the Dropbox folder on your Mac. (Dropbox [www.dropbox.com] is a free service that lets you share files easily across the Internet.)

Printopia works only on the Mac, but Windows users aren't left out in the cold. Collobos Software (www.collobos.com) has an application for the Mac and Windows PC called FingerPrint ($8 for the Mac and $10 for the Windows flavor). It does much of what Printopia does but runs as an application rather than as a service.

To print in either of these applications, you must have your computer turned on. When you do, your network printers appear, just as though they're natively compatible with AirPrint (**Figure 10.6**).

Figure 10.6
Printing from an iPhone with Printopia 2 installed on a Mac.

Troubleshooting

The iPhone and iPod touch may be engineering marvels, but even engineering marvels get moody from time to time, and when your device misbehaves, you're bound to be in a hurry to put things right. Allow me to lend a hand by suggesting the following troubleshooting techniques.

The basics

If your iPhone or iPod touch acts up in a general way—won't turn on, won't appear in iTunes, or quits and locks up—try these techniques.

No startup

Is your device just sitting there, with its cold black screen mocking you? Try charging it with an optional charger (perhaps you have one for an older iPod) rather than a USB 2.0 port. If you get no response after about 10 minutes, try another electrical outlet. Still nothing? Try a different sync cable.

Still no go, even though you've had that device for a long time and use it constantly? The battery may be dead (but this shouldn't happen in your first year of ownership, regardless of how much you use the thing).

No show in iTunes

If your iPhone or iPod touch doesn't appear in iTunes when you connect it to your computer, try these steps:

1. Make sure that your device is charged.

If the battery is dead, it may need about 10 minutes of charging before it can be roused enough to make an iTunes appearance.

2. Be sure that it's plugged into a USB 2.0 port.

Your computer won't recognize the device when it's attached to a USB 1.0 port or a FireWire port.

3. If you've configured it to sync wirelessly, be sure that you haven't ejected it from iTunes' Source list.

After you've attached your device to iTunes to enable Wi-Fi syncing (as I explain in Chapter 2) and then disconnected it, its icon still appears in iTunes' Source list. If you eject it by clicking the Eject button next to its icon in that Source list, iTunes no longer "sees" it. You must attach it to your computer again with a cable to make iTunes aware of its presence.

4. Plug your device into a different USB 2.0 port.

5. Unplug the iPhone or iPod touch, turn it off and then on, and plug it back in.

6. Throw the device into DFU mode (described in the nearby sidebar "The Four Rs").

7. Use a different syncing cable, if you have one.

8. Restart your computer, and try again.

9. Reinstall iTunes.

The Four Rs

In the following pages, I repeatedly refer to four troubleshooting techniques. In order of seriousness (and desirability), they are

- **Resign.** Force-quit the current app by holding down the Sleep/Wake button until the red Slide to Power Off slider appears. Then hold the Home button until you're taken to the Home screen. These steps should get you out of a frozen app.

  You can also try double-clicking the Home button to produce the Dock that contains recent apps. Tap and hold the app that's giving you problems until a small X appears in the icon's top-left corner; then tap the X to quit the app.

- **Restart.** Turn the device off and then on. Hold down the Sleep/Wake button until the Slide to Power Off slider appears. Do as the slider says, and slide it to the right; the iPhone or iPod touch shuts off. Now press the Sleep/Wake button to turn on the device.

- **Reset.** Press and hold the Home and Sleep/Wake buttons for about 10 seconds—until the Apple logo appears—and then let go. This step is akin to resetting your computer by holding down its power switch until it's forced to reboot.

(Continues on next page)

The Four Rs (continued)

- **Restore.** Plug your device into your computer, launch iTunes, select the iPhone or iPod touch in iTunes' Source list, click the Summary tab, and click the Restore button. This step wipes out all the data on your device and installs a clean version of its operating system.

If iTunes can't see the iPhone or iPod touch, you need to throw the phone into DFU (Device Firmware Upgrade) mode. To do that, plug the device into your computer with the USB cable, and press and hold the Sleep/Wake and Home buttons until you see the Apple logo. Then let go of the Sleep/Wake button and continue holding the Home button for 10 seconds. iTunes should tell you that the iPhone or iPod touch is in recovery mode, and you should be able to restore it.

Fortunately, iTunes makes a backup of your information data (contacts, calendar events, notes, apps, and so on) when it syncs the device. If you've chosen to back up your device to iCloud, you'll find your data there. If, after restoring from your backup, the device continues to misbehave, restore again—but this time when you're offered the chance to restore from a backup, choose to set it up as a new device.

Unresponsive (and uncooperative) apps

Just like the programs running on your computer, your apps—both those from Apple and third-party apps that you obtain from the App Store—can act up, freezing or quitting unexpectedly. You can try a few things to nudge your iPhone or iPod touch into action. If the first step doesn't work, march to the next.

1. Resign from the app.

If an app refuses to do anything, it's likely frozen. The only way to thaw it is to force it to quit. Press and hold the Sleep/Wake button until the Slide to Power Off slider appears; then click and hold the Home button until you're taken to the Home screen. Alternatively, quit the app via the recent-apps Dock, as I describe in the sidebar "The Four Rs."

2. Restart your device.

   Some apps misbehave until you shut down the iPhone or iPod touch and then restart it.

3. Clear Safari's cache.

   If you find that Safari quits suddenly, something in its cache may be corrupted, and clearing the cache may solve the problem. To do so, tap Settings > Safari, and in the Safari settings screen, tap Clear Cookies and Data.

4. Reset the device by holding down the Home and Sleep/Wake buttons until you see the Apple logo.

5. Delete and reinstall troublesome third-party apps.

   If a third-party app quits time and again, tap and hold its icon until it and the other icons start wiggling. Tap the X in the app icon's top-left corner to remove it from the device. Go to the App Store, locate the app, and download it again. Apple keeps a record of your app purchases, so you won't have to pay for it again.

6. On the iPhone or iPod touch, go to the General setting; tap Reset; and then tap Reset All Settings.

   This step resets the device's preferences but doesn't delete any of your data or media.

7. In that same Reset screen, tap Erase All Content and Settings and then confirm by tapping the resulting Erase button (**Figure 10.7**).

Figure 10.7
Erasing all the content and settings on your device is the nearly next-to-last resort.

> **tip** This step vaporizes not only the device's preferences, but its data and media content as well; you're essentially left with a device that behaves like it just came out of the box. Before doing this, try to sync your iPhone or iPod touch so that you can save any events, contacts, bookmarks, and photos you've created, as well as the third-party apps.

> **note** You want to try to back up third-party apps in particular because all the data for those apps is stored within the apps themselves.

8. Restore the device.

As I suggest in the sidebar "The Four Rs," restore from your backup. If the problem persists, something in the backup may be corrupted.

9. Plug it into your computer and restore yet again, but choose *not* to restore from a backup; instead, start as though you're configuring a new device.

iTunes will install everything afresh—including a fresh copy of iOS, which means that you'll have to resync your data.

Index

Unlimited online access to all Peachpit, Ad
Press, Apple Training and New Riders vide
and books, as well as content from other
leading publishers including: O'Reilly Med
Focal Press, Sams, Que, Total Training, Joh
Wiley & Sons, Course Technology PTR, Cla
on Demand, VTC and more.

No time commitment or contract requi
Sign up for one month or a year.
All for $19.99 a month

SIGN UP TODAY
peachpit.com/creativeedge